Published by Periplus Editions (HK) Ltd.
with editorial offices at
130 Joo Seng Road #06-01
Singapore 368357

Copyright © 2002
Periplus Editions (HK) Ltd.

ISBN: 962-593-026-4

Library of Congress
Card Number: 2002101482

Photo credits
All food photography by Masano Kawana.
Additional photos by Masano Kawana (endpaper, pages
1, 12–13, 15, 19–21, 23); Craig J. Brown (pages 2, 4, 6–11,
14, 16–18; J.M. Leenders (page 22); Luca Invernizzi
Tettoni (page 3).

-Distributed by

USA
Tuttle Publishing
364 Innovation Drive
North Clarendon, VT 05759 9436
Tel: (802) 773-8930
Fax: (802) 773-6993

Japan and Korea
Tuttle Publishing
RK Building 2nd Floor 2-13-10
Shimo-Meguro, Meguro-Ku
Tokyo 153 0064, Japan
Tel: (81-3) 5437-0171
Fax: (81-3) 5437-0755

Asia Pacific
Berkeley Books Pte Ltd.
130 Joo Seng Road #06-01
Singapore 368357
Tel: (65) 6280-1330
Fax: (65) 6280-6290

First Edition
1 3 5 7 9 10 8 6 4 2
09 08 07 06 05 04 03 02
PRINTED IN SINGAPORE

THE FOOD OF
KOREA

Authentic Recipes from the Land of Morning Calm

Texts by David Clive Price
Recipes by chefs of The Shilla Hotel, Seoul
Photos by Masano Kawana
Styling by Christina Ong
Prop styling by Kim Kyung Mi

PERIPLUS

Contents

Part One: Food in Korea

Geography, climate, and history
have all shaped Korea's cuisine.

Many factors have contributed to the evolution of Korean cooking over the centuries, and the most important of these are the geography and climate, the importance of medicinal vegetables and herbs, and the various influences that have presented themselves throughout the history of this land.

The Korean peninsula juts out like a spur from the Asian mainland, just below Manchuria in northeastern China, and eastern Siberia. Approximately the size of the United Kingdom, it stretches 620 miles (1,000 kilometers) north to south, but is only 135 miles (216 kilometers) east to west at its narrowest point. To the west lies the Yellow Sea and China; to the east the East Sea and Japan. Scattered off the jagged coastline are some 3,000 islands.

But apart from the encircling sea, Korea is a land of mountains. An enduring image of this Land of Morning Calm is of wave upon wave of blue mountains, their peaks rising through the morning mist. Only 20 percent of the country consists of arable land, and of this a large proportion is represented by the rice-growing Honam plain in southwest Korea. The east coast, ribbed by the magnificent Diamond Mountains, falls abruptly to the East Sea. The west coast is riddled with shallow, narrow inlets that experience large tidal changes. Between these coasts the peninsula is ribboned with swift-flowing rivers originating in the mountains.

In addition to water, the country is rich in forests. An extensive reforestation program was begun after the Korean War and now the mountain parks are full of juniper, bamboo, willow, red maples, and flowering fruit and nut trees such as apricot, pear, peach, plum, cherry, persimmon, chestnut, walnut, ginkgo, and pine nut. Autumn in the Sorak mountains of the east coast or spring at Kyongju, ancient capital of Unified Korea, brings a marvel of foliage in varying hues.

Korea has four distinct seasons: spring and autumn are temperate, winter and summer verge on the extremes. Winter is particularly cold, with temperatures dropping to 24°F (-15°C) or less, and it often lasts from November until late March. This climate, in combination with the mountainous interior, has given Koreans an appetite for hearty, stimulating food, which helps to keep out the cold and produce energy—meat, soup, chilies, garlic, ginseng, and many medicinal vegetables, berries, and nuts. At the same time, the four seasons have guaranteed the Koreans a steady flow of seasonal produce. The lowland fields provide excellent grains and vegetables, while the uplands grow wild

Page 2:
Colorful masks and participants at the Pongsan Talchum dance at the Andong Mask Festival.

Opposite:
A selection of vegetarian fare, served at Sanchon restaurant in Insadong.

Squid being prepared to be hung and dried off Ulleung Island.

Koreans often look to herbal remedies for illnesses, the result of their grounding in Chinese medical belief about the yin-yang balance of the body and the warming-cooling properties of certain foods. The most common medicinal foods used in cooking are dried persimmon, jujube (red dates), pine seeds, chestnut, ginkgo, tangerine, and ginseng. The sapodin in garlic, which Koreans often eat raw wrapped in a lettuce leaf round barbecued meat, is said to cleanse the blood and aid digestion. Chicken and pork are considered the first steps to obesity, so are largely avoided. Nuts are supposed to be good for pregnancy as well as the skin; jujube and bellflower root for coughs and colds; raw potato juice for an upset stomach; while dried pollack with bean sprouts and tofu is said to be good for hangovers.

Much of Korean history was characterized by the struggle between the supporters of Buddhism and Confucianism for control of the system of patronage; this consequently also greatly influenced the food.

The Silla kingdom, based on Kyongju, united the Korean nation for the first time in the seventh century, giving birth to a long period of Buddhist culture. This culture continued to flourish into the Koryo dynasty (AD 935–1368). However, although Koryo patronized Buddhism and the monks played an important role in national affairs, the Koryo kings also adopted Confucian-style government bureaucracy and civil service examinations from China. By the time Ghenghis Khan's Mongol alliance invaded Korea in 1231, the Koryo court had become torn between Confucian reform and the age-old Buddhist cultural heritage. A treaty made with China in 1279

and cultivated mushrooms, roots, and greens. The surrounding seas produce a host of fish, seafood, seaweed, and crustaceans. However, it is the sense of food as medicine and long-term protection that has governed the evolution of the Korean diet. Even raw fish *sashimi* is given extra vitality by being seasoned with red chili. Most meals are served with a gruel or a soup, as well as the ubiquitous, fortifying kimchi and a range of vegetarian side dishes collectively known as *namul*, which are delicately seasoned with soy, seasame, and garlic.

gave Koryo semi-autonomy but required Korean princes to reside in the new Mongol capital at Beijing; they also had to marry Mongol princesses.

When the Ming dynasty was established in China in 1368, and the Mongols were driven out, Koryo looked like the next prize on the list. However, the invading armies of the Ming Chinese were driven back by Yi Sog-gye, a fiery Korean commander who deposed the king of Koryo and invoked the Mandate of Heaven to establish his own Yi dynasty.

The Yi dynasty lasted over 500 years and ended only with the annexation of Korea by Japan in 1910. Yi's first king was wily enough to re-establish tributary relations with China and also to adopt Confucianism as the state creed, renaming his kingdom Chosun, after China's ancient name for Korea. From then onwards, Confucianism steadily replaced Buddhism in national life; in effect, Buddhism was outlawed to Korea's mountain temples.

There, close to the forests and mountain streams, Buddhist monks continued to study the scriptures; they also developed a "mountain cuisine" that has become the foundation of Korean cooking today. For example, meat, which is forbidden to the Buddhist monk, and anything that is strong smelling, such as garlic and scallion, did not feature in temple cuisine. While modern Korean Buddhism is not so rigid about garlic, this cuisine has retained its traditional dependence on roots, grasses, and herbs. Today, the visitor to any temples from Seoraksan in the northeast to Chirisan in the south is greeted by piles of mushrooms, roots, and medicinal herbs on sale at the entrance. A typical temple meal consists of soup, rice, and *namul,* which is gathered from the woods and hills.

The collected roots and grasses are then prepared simply with soy sauce, crushed garlic, sesame seeds and oil, and seasonings. The preparation of *namul* varies from region to region, but the dishes are exactly the same as the side dishes of *namul* that accompany family and restaurant meals in Korean cities and towns, consisting of appetizers of shepherd's purse, mugwort, parsely, and sow thistle; *namul* of wild aster, bracken, royal fern, marsh plant, day lily, aralia roots, and bellflower, to name just a few.

Other stalwarts of the Korean table originate from the mountains, too, such as vegetable pancakes or *jeon,* which are usually filled with lentils or leeks and are sometimes fashioned in the shape of a flower.

Harvesting of rice by hand in the Gyungsnanbukdo Province in autumn.

A Culinary Tour of the Peninsula

South Korea's regional foods offer tastes and culinary experiences as colorful as Korea's temple-filled valleys and rocky bays

The Kyonggido province surrounding Seoul offers rice and grain farmlands, vegetables from the eastern mountains, and seafood from the Yellow Sea. Its simple fare, served in generous, rather unspicy portions, includes Beef Rib Soup (*Galbitang*), made of well-marbled short ribs boiled for as long as it takes to draw out the marrow; Beef Stock Soup (*Gomtang*), boiled with beef entrails and radishes; and the springtime Shepherd's Pouch Soup (*Naengiguk*), boiled with soybean paste, hot chili paste, and clams.

By contrast, the rugged Kangwondo province to the east provides abundant seafood due to the crossing of warm and cold currents in the East Sea. The region is mountainous, and offers many kinds of cereals, corn, and potatoes. The fare is unsophisticated but healthy, including Stuffed Squid (*Ojingoh Sundae*) with bean curd and vegetables from tiny Ullungdo Island; Mud Fish Stew (*Chuohtang*), made with mud fish, potatoes, leeks and mushrooms; Fried Potato Pancakes (*Gamjajeon*), mixed with chopped leeks, scallions, and green chilies, which is a speciality of the snowy Seoraksan and Odaesan national parks; and Cold Buckwheat Noodles (*Memil Makguksu*) at Chuncheon, the provincial capital, delicately spiced with kimchi juice and cold beef stock.

Chungcheong-do province is divided between between its south coast and a northern landlocked part. South Chungcheong harvests sumptuous marine products from plentiful fishing grounds in the Yellow Sea, while North Chungcheong produces many kinds of mountain vegetables. Delicacies, which are mainly mild and savory, include Boiled Rice with assorted mountain vegetables and mushrooms (*Sanchae Pyogo Bibimbap*) picked from Mount Songni; Acorn Jelly (*Dotorimuk*) with acorn pancake and cold acorn noodles as variations; Grilled Todok (*Deodeok Gui*), a pounded mountain root seasoned with red-pepper paste sauce and grilled on a griddle; and Pickled Crab (*Kkogejang*), marinated crabs in soy sauce mixed with red chili, garlic, and sesame oil.

Opposite:
A fishing village on Ulleung Island.

Left:
Squid being hung to dry in the sun at Namho village on the east coast.

Kyonsangdo, centered around the southeastern industrial city of Taegu, the port city of Pusan and the ancient capital of Kyongju, produces abundant crops and marine products all year round. The hot and salty dishes include Taegu Soup (*Taegutang*), in which beef is cooked with Chinese cabbage, bracken, and scallion; Large Clam Gruel (*Daehap Juk*), boiled with sticky rice, jujube, and ginseng; Steamed Big-Mouth Fish (*Agutchim*), fished from the port of Masan and dried, seasoned, and steamed with watercress and bean sprouts until the bones soften; and Sashimi (*Saengson Hoe*) with sea trout, flatfish, flounder, sweetfish, and greenling caught from the East and South Seas and served with sour red chili paste sauce.

A typical galbi *dinner at a street restaurant in Seoul.*

Pusan boasts a magnificent early morning fish market at Jagalchi, and its *sashimi* restaurants—mainly a species of striped canvas tents that are lit at night like fortune teller booths—stretch along the craggy shoreline, offering a cornucopia of raw fish, spicy sauces, and *soju* (wine made using potato and rice).

Kyongju's seasonal fruits, such as pears, apples, and persimmons, together with acorn jelly and jellyfish mustard salad, form the backdrop to several colorful, bright tasting seasonal recipes.

A varied and luxurious cuisine has been developed from the sumptuous products of the fertile Honam plain and the seas lying to the south and west of the province of Jeollado. This area is famous for the large number of side dishes served at one meal—particularly in the many traditional farmhouses—and for a unique kimchi. But perhaps the most famous Jeolla dish is Jeonju Rice Hash (*Jeonju Bibimbap*), the precursor of and model for all *bibimbap* dishes in Korea. Shredded beef, soya bean sprouts, dried mushrooms, bellflower root, and bracken are mixed with soy sauce, garlic, and sesame oil, and sautéed until brown. The ingredients are then mixed together in a large bowl, a fried egg is placed on top, and a bowl of rice is upended into the mixture.

In Jeonju, five different variations of kimchi and *namul* are placed on the table, along with big green peppers. The rice, which is cooked in wood and iron braziers, is mixed with a dark soy and onion sauce and served with ginseng root spread with kimchi and barbecued on the grill. The dish sets the body on fire, and the best restaurant for it in Jeonju is the Chungang Hoekwan.

Jeollado also offers Seasoned Broiled Eel (*Jangeo Gui*), a tonic dish in hot summer weather seasoned with red-pepper paste sauce; Seasoned Broiled

Octopus (*Nakchi Gui*), octopus tentacles wrapped in straw and broiled; and Jeollado Kimchi, a savory kimchi of rich seafood ingredients. In addition to napa (Chinese) cabbage, the ingredients used in this kimchi are Korean lettuce, leaf mustard, welsh onion, radish leaves, bean sprouts, eggplant, and green pepper.

The romantic honeymooners' island of Jeju off the southern coast has limited cultivable land but well stocked waters. It produces mainly cereals and sweet potatoes, rather than rice. The straightforward nature of the inhabitants is reflected in their food, in which seasonings are used sparingly.

Local specialities include Abalone Porridge (*Jeonbokjuk*), thin slices of abalone fried with sesame oil and then mixed with rice and water before being simmered in a pot seasoned with salt (Jeju abalone used to be offered to the king as a tribute); Seafood Earthen-pot Stew (*Haemul Ttukpaegi*), boiled without vegetables but enriched with clams, oysters, sea-urchin eggs, and soybean paste; Stone-pot Boiled Rice with Mushrooms (*Dolsot Pyogo Bibimbap*), consisting of

A restaurant patron enjoying a dinner of Ssambapchip.

rice boiled with *pyogo* mushrooms and mountain vegetables picked from the slopes of Mount Halla and served on a hot stone-pot; and Mixed Black Sea-bream Sashimi (*Jarimulhoe*), Jeju's unique black bream sliced without removing its bones and mixed with scallions, watercress, cucumber, Chinese pepper, and cold water.

But equally, no one should visit Jeju without tasting a dish of fresh oysters, plucked from the sea by Jeju's famous women oyster divers, an example of the island's rapidly vanishing matriarchal society. Jeju also grows oranges and has its own herds of cattle.

Finally, Seoul, the capital of Korea for 600 years and the third largest city in the world, offers many kinds of regional and metropolitan cuisine. The abundance of foodstuffs brought in from every corner of the country has ensured a remarkable variety of recipes, and because of the influence of the royal family and aristocracy, the city boasts elegant table settings and skilful cooking. Much of this old court cuisine has been passed down to the Korean people.

Beef Rice Soup (*Seolleongtang*), for example, which is made by boiling beef entrails and bones for a whole day, was eaten by the king and the people together after ceremonial prayers for a good harvest. The ceremony was performed at the Sollong Altar in central Seoul, hence the name.

Beef Rib Stew (*Galbi Jjim*) is another Seoul specialty, and visitors to the kitchens of traditional Seoul restaurants will often find a huge pot of water, sugar, rice wine, ground pear, radish, carrots, ginkgo nuts, cinnamon, and chestnuts boiling away, ready for preparing the *galbi*. *Galbi* ribs are cut off the bone in longtitudinal, unfolded sections, scored and seasoned before being broiled on a grill.

Barbecued Beef (*Bulgogi*) is perhaps one of the best known of Korean foods, and it is particularly associated with Seoul. For this dish, a tenderloin or sirloin of beef is sliced thinly, scored lightly to make it more tender, then marinated with sugar, rice wine, garlic, sesame oil, and soybean sauce, and finally barbecued over a charcoal fire. It is often accompanied by lettuce leaves, raw whole garlic, and scallions.

Seoul also offers a Spicy Beef Soup (*Yukgaejang*) for Koreans enervated by the humid summer heat. Brisket of beef is deeply broiled and seasoned with hot spices, so much so that people perspire when they eat it, illustrating the Korean's philosophy of "fighting heat with heat."

On New Year's Day, a Sliced Rice Cake Soup (*Tteokguk*) is eaten. This is a beef broth in which hardened bars of rice cake are thinly sliced and boiled until almost swollen. More recently, another of Seoul's specialities—the ubiquitous *mandu*, or Chinese dumplings—has been added to the broth instead of rice cake. Dumplings are one of several Chinese influences on Korean food, epitomizing its eclectic nature.

Kimchi, Spices, and Ginseng

The obligatory elements that contribute to the
vigor and idiosyncracy of Korean food

"A man can live without a wife but not without kimchi" is an old Korean saying. "As Korean as kimchi" is another. Even today it is virtually impossible to find a Korean house, apartment, or monastery without rows of big, black enameled kimchi pots on the porch or balcony, or, in the snowy months, beneath the earth.

Kimchi can be preserved for a long time. Its hot and spicy taste stimulates the appetite, and it is nutritious, providing vitamins, lactic acid, and minerals otherwise lacking in the winter diet. The introduction of chili into the pickling process of vegetables in the 17th century, a process that dates back a thousand years or more, was an important innovation in Korean food culture. Using chilies in combination with vegetables and fish resulted in a unique method of food preservation and led to the adoption of kimchi as a Korean staple.

Red chili and garlic are the mainstays of the basic kimchi formula, which calls for heads of fresh cabbage to be cut open, salted, placed in brine with lots of red chili and garlic and set to ferment. In summer, when fermentation is rapid, kimchi is made fresh every day. In winter, the big kimchi pots are packed in straw and buried in the earth to prevent freezing, then left to ferment for months. There are literally hundreds of kimchi types. There is even a Myongga Kimchi Museum in Seoul that displays them! However, the most common variants are: Wrapped Kimchi (*Bossam* Kimchi), comprising seafood such as octopus, shrimp, and oyster; White Cabbage Kimchi (*Baek* Kimchi), mainly made in the south and containing pickled fish, and sometimes eaten with noodles in winter; Stuffed Cucumber Kimchi (*Oisobaegi*), made with cucumbers stuffed with seasonings; Hot Radish Kimchi (*Kkaktugi*), made with Korean white radishes cut into small cubes, seasoned and fermented; "Bachelor" Radish Kimchi (*Chonggak* Kimchi), made with small salted white radishes and anchovies; and Sliced Radish and Cabbage Kimchi (*Nabak* Kimchi), with small pieces of white radish

Opposite:
Freshly planted ginseng fields in central Korea, near the Maisan provincial park, in early autumn.

Left:
Leek on sale at an auction market in Seoul.

or cabbage pickled in seasoned brine, mixed with whole green or red chilies, and served chilled.

Besides red chili and garlic, favourite Korean seasonings include scallions or Korean leek, ginger, sesame oil, sesame seeds, rice wine, and soy sauce. Cooking herbs are used on account of their association with traditional herbal medicine. There are also many fermented pastes and sauces for dipping, called *chang*. Every restaurant and home has its own formula for making *chang*. Based on a fermented mash of soy beans, the three most common varieties are *kan chang* (dark and liquid), *daen chang* (thick and pungent), and *gochu chang* (fiery and hot).

Ginseng (*insam*) is also a staple of the Korean diet; it is also one of Korea's most universally recognized symbols. Due to the root's uncanny resemblance to the anthropoid human form, the Chinese characters that denote ginseng are made up of "man" and "root."

Chinese experiments with herbal medicine go back 5,500 years to the Emperor Shen Nung. The earliest medical texts that are known to have survived give ample mention of ginseng, and in medicine, as in many other fields, Korea proved to be China's earliest and best pupil. There is evidence of Chinese medicinal herbs being trans-

planted into Korea during the third century BC, and Chinese medical texts have always been widely perused by Korean scholars and healers. By the mid-17th century, the Dutchman Hendrick Hamel could describe ginseng as a plant indigenous to Korea. Originally found in remote wild mountains in northern Korea, ginseng is now cultivated throughout the peninsula, especially on Kanghwa Island. The roots are grown in long, neat rows protected from the elements by thatched shelters. After harvesting, they are washed, peeled, and dried, then sorted according to age and quality into white ginseng types. Red ginseng, which is regarded by Koreans as the very best, is steamed before being dried in the sun, which is believed to increase its medicinal powers.

Koreans consume an enormous amount of ginseng—as root, pills, capsules, candies, chewing gum, cigarettes, tonics, and beauty products. Ginseng tea (*insam-cha*) is a national drink, and is available in tea shops everywhere. Perhaps the most famous ginseng dish is Ginseng Chicken Soup (*Samgyetang*). The chicken is stuffed with ginseng, jujube, sticky rice, and garlic, then stewed. The result is a sweet, tender, flavorsome dish that is sublimely cooling on hot summer days.

Liquors and Tea

Drinking etiquette and the way of tea
help enhance social relations between Koreans

Drinking has always played an important role in Korean leisure life, especially at the royal court. Many of the oldest ceramics excavated in Korea are drinking cups and liquor vessels, and there are many references to drinking parties in Korean literature and art. Drinking is a national pastime today, and there is no better way for the visitor to delve beneath the veneer of Korean society and get to know Koreans than by drinking with them in a typical liquor house (*sul-jip*).

Etiquette on drinking occasions includes several traditional customs. When being served by an elder person, the glass is held in both hands. The face is slightly turned away while drinking, and the contents are enjoyed slowly. When the glass is returned to the elder person, it is held in the right hand with the left hand supporting the right elbow gently. During pouring, the bottle is held in the right hand and the left hand supports the right elbow.

Such Confucian-style rules sound extremely cumbersome but it is surprising how relaxed and graceful they can make one feel. Drinking in Korea is a social experience and there is a whole range of Korean liquors, tonics, and teas to enjoy. Ginseng liquor (*insam-sul*), for example, is prepared by leaving a whole ginseng root to soak in a bottle of *soju*, a Korean gin made from potatoes, best enjoyed with Ginseng Chicken.

Soju leaves a bad hangover if taken in excess, and the best remedy is a ginseng tonic. A more acceptable version is *makgeolli*, a milky white brew fermented from rice, said to be highly nutritious. There are many traditional *makgeolli* drinking establishments in Seoul and the provincial cities. These are well worth a visit for their old-fashioned wooden decor, the snacks (*anju*) they serve, and their air of conviviality. *Popchu*, a high-grade rice wine similar to Japanese *sake* and usually served hot, is a specialty of Konju, central Korea. Beer has become increasingly popular in Korea, especially the bottled variety, while draught beer can be found in the many beer halls (*tong-dalkjip*) specializing in broiled chicken.

Koreans never drink without *anju*. These snacks absorb the alcohol and create a thirst. Favorite *anju* are soybean curd; raw crab legs marinated in red chili sauce; sliced raw fish; fish roe in garlic sauce; blanched spinach dressed with sesame oil and seeds, dried anchovies sautéed with red chilies; broiled fish sprinkled with sesame seeds; green garlic pickled in soy sauce; sautéed oysters, beef and bean curd patties spiced with ginger; mung bean pancake laced with shrimp; and ground beef patties with garlic and sesame seeds.

The history of tea drinking in Korea mirrors the rise and fall of Buddhism in the country. Tea invigorates one's mind and was popular with Buddhist monks and followers. The practice then declined under Confucianism but has since been revived and is enjoyed throughout the land.

A variety of delicious teas are usually served with traditional Korean cuisine, but not all are from the tea plant. Koreans prefer teas brewed from grains, dried fruits, and ginseng. Popular teas today include barley tea (*bori-cha*)—the national beverage whch is served free of charge at every restaurant and tea room in the country, and which is often served cold in homes—quince tea (*mogwa-cha*), walnut tea (*hodo-cha*), ginseng tea (*insam-cha*), citron tea (*yuja-cha*), jujube tea (*daechu-cha*), and roasted corn tea (*oksusu-cha*).

Green tea (*nok-cha*) was the first tea introduced to Korea, arriving during the reign of Queen Seondeok (AD 632-647) of the Silla Kingdom (57 BC–AD 935). Annual green tea festivals are still held in green tea plantations in Boseonggun, Jeollanamdo, and Hadonggun, Gyeongsangnamdo.

Tea houses in Korea offer a wide variety of teas in elegant antique interiors against a backdrop of traditional Koeran music. Free tea tastings are sometimes also conducted. Sweet desserts to be served with tea, particularly on festive occasions, include deep fried cereals (*yugwa*); roots or fruits stewed in honey or sugar syrup (*jeongwa*); honey-nut nougat; and steamed rice and nuts in sesame oil and honey (*dasik*).

Table Settings and Etiquette

Koreans have different table settings depending on the occasion, the main dish, and the number of side dishes.

Korean table settings are classified into 3-*cheop*, 5-*cheop*, 7-*cheop*, 9-*cheop*, and 12-*cheop*, according to the number of side dishes served at a meal. For an everyday Korean meal, the average family takes about four side dishes, along with rice—traditionally the center of all table arrangements—soup, and kimchi. The main meals include breakfast, which is the most fortifying meal of the day, a lighter lunch (called *jeomsin*, which means "to lighten the heart"), and a not-too-heavy dinner.

A 12-cheop table setting, traditionally served only to royalty, now offered by the Sorabol restaurant at The Shilla Hotel.

The basic *bansang* setting includes seven side dishes with boiled rice, soup, three seasoning sauces—such as red chili paste, kimchi, and hot radish kimchi—and two heavier soups, such as hot pollack or rib stew. These soups are considered an accompaniment to the meal and not a starter. Except for the individual bowl of rice and soup, the dishes are shared.

The younger diners are expected to wait for their elders and not leave the table before the latter members do. Rice, soup, and stews are eaten with spoons, and the rather dry side dishes are eaten with metal chopsticks, but spoon and chopsticks are not used at the same time. Bowls and plates are also not raised from the table.

A traditional Korean meal will be served at a low table on the *ondol* floor, which provides heating in the winter months, and the diners will be seated on cushions.

The ceremonial aspect of Korean dining has been greatly influenced by Confucianism and the royal court. There are abundant archives of royal dishes in Korea, and some of them can still be experienced in their entirety. For example, *Gujeolpan* (Nine-sectioned Royal Platter) is served in an octagonal lacquered platter with nine compartments. Delicate pancakes are placed in the center, surrounded by eight other treasures to be carefully interwoven into the pancakes. Another royal delicacy is *Shinseolo*, which means "the food of hermits in fairyland" and which comes in a brass pot with a chimney, rather like a Mongolian fire-pot. The hotpot is served with blanched walnuts and fried ginkgo nuts after being simmered in its own broth. The cuisine of the royal court is the basis for an elaborate à la carte presentation of foods called *Teuk-byeol Yori* or "specialities," which range from appetizers to rice cakes and cookies.

Many festivals in Korea are based on the lunar calendar, and the food prepared for these festivals is appropriate to the season as well as being symbolic. The New Year's Day Table, following a Confucian ceremony honoring one's ancestors, includes sweet rice, three-colored vegetables, and *Gujeolpan*. The first full moon of the year is celebrated with all-night games and fun, dry vegetables from the previous year, and five kinds of grains—plain and glutinous rice, millet, corn, and red beans—in a special dish. Wine is also drunk to prevent deafness.

Chuseok, or Thanksgiving for the newly harvested rice, is marked by rice cakes in a half-moon shape and by five grains, both of which are a mark of respect to ancestors. On Ancestor's Memorial Day, food is presented at the grave site and eaten there. On Buddha's Birthday mountain vegetables are the main dish of the day, while on the Baby's First Birthday, a brush and paint, books and thread are placed on the table to pray for the baby's long and fruitful life. Other culinary festivities include preparing evil-dispelling pounded rice cakes on January 1st, and glutinous rice cakes with angelika petals on the Buddhist festival of hair-washing. At Confucian and shamanist ceremonies, an offering is made of a pig's head stuffed with money.

Traditional Korean-style settings exemplified in The Shilla Hotel in Seoul. This is a table set for one, the master of the house.

A Bride's Gift Table comprises stuffed jujubes, broiled beef patties, chestnuts, a nine-sectioned dish, wine, and chicken in tasseled handkerchiefs, while a 61st Birthday Table is a large feast served because the lunar calendar has reached its span of 60 years and is set to begin again. The Korean people thus celebrate the passing of each season with a full culinary calendar, fruit of their Buddhist Confucian background and rich agricultural heritage.

Part Two: Cooking in Korea

Despite the modern electric stove, some traditional food preparation methods are still preferred.

In traditional Korean kitchens, cooks prepared dishes over a wood fire but in modern times, the gas and electric stove is the norm. Apart from a couple of unusual cooking or serving instruments, most of the important utensils are very common. A good, heavy skillet is recommended, as is a wok for stir-frying, and some sturdy saucepans and casseroles are essential.

Koreans, like most East Asians, eat a lot of rice. In ancient times they ate millet, and Koreans are not averse to adding other grains to their rice, like millet, or black (soy) beans. Korean rice is short grain, similar to the rice favored by the Japanese. To cook rice on a regular basis, a modern electric rice cooker is a must.

The Korean barbecue is well-known throughout the world and in Korea it is a popular way of cooking beef in restaurants and in street stalls. At home, families usually use a table-top grill on which to cook *bulgogi* and *galbi* ribs.

Many families also own a special pot used in steamboat or firekettle meals. This unusual vessel has a central chimney surrounded by a moat which is filled with morsels of food and kept in the fridge until ready to eat. An hour or more before mealtime, coals are lit in an outside barbecue so that when the vessel is removed from the fridge and placed at the dining area, the glowing red coals can be inserted into the chimney. A hot broth is poured into the moat and is kept hot by the chimney. Diners are then able to select food items from the hot broth—this is a delicious and very social way of dining!

Visitors to the Korean kitchen will no doubt notice an array of eathernware crocks or storage jars. These are not for display but are used, even today, to store and ferment Korean foods such as *ganjang* (soy sauce), *gochujang* (Korean-chili paste), *deonjang* (fermented soybean paste), and kimchi. The pots keep their contents from going bad and are able to keep kimchi fresh for a long time.

The *jangdokdae* is the place where Koreans place the pots used to store fermented food. It is usually located in the backyard near the kitchen in a high area with plenty of sunshine and good ventilation. It is traditional for soybean pastes and sauces to be made in the spring while the process of kimchi making is usually begun in the fall.

Opposite:
A traditional Korean kitchen features a fire oven.

This page:
Kimchi urn, steamer, and stoneware pot.

Korean Ingredients

Essential ingredients to achieve the true tastes of Korea

Asian pear and Citron

Bracken

Crown daisy

Dallae

ABALONE: A highly prized shellfish in Korea and much of Asia, abalone must be sliced thinly and tenderized before cooking. Cook very quickly or simmer for a long time; anything in between will result in tough flesh.

ANCHOVIES: All sizes of dried anchovies are used in Korean cuisine, from the tiny to the large. The smaller ones are often used to make fried anchovies in soy sauce, while the larger ones are preferred for making broth. They are readily available from Asian food stores.

ASIAN PEAR: Also known as Oriental pear, apple pear, or *nashi*, the Asian pear resembles an apple but tastes like a pear. It is crunchy, juicy, and very fragrant, and can be cooked or served raw.

BAMBOO SHOOTS: If using canned bamboo shoots, drain and boil in water for 10 minutes to remove any metallic taste.

BARLEY: Used to make the popular barley punch (*sikhye*), the millet is slowly boiled in water and then discarded; the resultant flavored barley water is then mixed with other ingredients.

BEAN CURD: Also known as *dubu* in Korea, both the firm Chinese-style bean curd and the Japanese softer bean curd are popular.

BEAN SPROUTS : Sprouted green mung beans can be stored in the refrigerator for abut 2 to 3 days. They are used in soups, salads, and fried dishes.

BRACKEN: Also known as fiddlehead or fern tip. This is an edible fern about 7 inches long with the rounded violinlike head curled in a tight circle. Bracken is available throughout the year.

BELLFLOWER ROOT: Also known as *toraji*. To remove the bitterness, fresh bellflower roots are steeped in brine or rubbed with salt, or they are tossed in chili powder, leek, and garlic; and then fermented. Omit if not available.

BELL PEPPER: Also known as capsicum, red and green bell peppers are a frequent addition to many Korean dishes.

BLUE SWIMMER CRAB: One of the most common types of crab, the blue swimmer crab can be found all over the world.

CILANTRO: The fresh leaves and stems of the coriander plant are a popular seasoning item. Substitute with Chinese parsley.

CITRON: Thinly sliced citron peel is the main flavoring in Korean citron tea. Korean citron is rather sour, has a strong fragrance, and contains a large amount of vitamin C.

CHILI: See Korean chili.

COURGETTE: See Zucchini.

CROWN DAISY: The leaves of this variety of

chrysanthemum are not bitter but can have a strong grassy smell. They are used in Korean recipes as a kind of spinach.

CUCUMBER: This is a common vegetable on the Korean table. Cucumbers are normally not peeled in Korean cuisine. Choose young, slender cucumbers with thin skins.

DALLAE: Also known as wild rocambole, this plant has been known to be a therapeutic plant from the earliest times. Omit if not available.

DRIED POLLACK: This is a small variety of cod. The roe is popular preserved with salt and ground chili pepper.

EGGPLANT: Try to use the long, slender Japanese-style eggplants (aubergines), and not the more bulbous Western variety, which tends to be too bitter and requires salting before use.

FERMENTED SHRIMPS: Fermented, or pickled, shrimps is a popular condiment, while the juice is used in the preparation of some dishes. It has a pungent smell and strong taste.

FERMENTED SOYBEAN PASTE: One of the most important seasonings in the Korean kitchen, fermented soybean paste (*deonjang*) is usually made at home in earthernware crocks or storage pots. Made from fermented soy bean cakes, red chili, and salt, this paste is available from Korean food stores and markets. This paste lasts a long time, in fact it matures with age somewhat akin to wine. It is not unusual for families to keep homemade *deonjang* for 20 or more years.

GARLIC: As well as being used to flavor dishes, raw garlic cloves are often eaten together with grilled, marinated meat wrapped in a lettuce leaf.

GINGER: Try to find fresh young or mature ginger rather than dried, powdered ginger, which does not possess the same intense flavor.

GINSENG ROOT: A highly prized medicinal root believed to have rejuvenating properties, ginseng is widely cultivated in Korea and used extensively in Korean cooking. It tastes similar to parsnip, and is used in soups, stews, and teas. It is very expensive. For some recipes, however, such as ginseng tea, it is not necessary to use whole aged ginseng, so try looking for the cheaper alternative—packets of younger, creamy white dried rootlets. Available from Asian food stores and medicine halls.

JUJUBE: Also known as dried red date, this sun-dried fruit is not really a date. It is native to the Mediterranean and China, and is used in both sweet and savory dishes as a flavoring.

KELP: Also known as *konbu*, kelp is a kind of dried dark-brown seaweed, sold in folded sheets. Thicker than laver, it expands into smooth, green sheets in liquid and is added to dishes only for its flavor and color; it is usually discarded after cooking.

KIMCHI: Korea's favorite food, kimchi is made by pickling vegetables with chilies, garlic, ginger, other vegetables and seasonings and allowing the mixture to mature. This staple comes in many varieties, but the most common is napa (Chinese) cabbage pickled with ingredients such as red chili flakes, garlic, onion juice, and ginger. If you do not wish to make your own, kimchi can also be purchased in jars from

Dried pollack

Fermented shrimps

Jujube

3 types of Korean chili

Korean watercress

Leek

Napa cabbage

Pine nuts

Korean grocers. No Korean meal is complete without kimchi.

KOREAN CHILI: Also known as *gochu*, the red chili is widely used in Korean cooking to prepare kimchi and many hot soups and stews. **Chili flakes** are made by coarsely crushing seeded, dried red chilies. **Chili powder** is first seeded, then ground to a fine powder. The powder is used as a color and to distribute heat uniformly in kimchi. The dried seeds are also occasionally used in kimchi. **Chili threads** are dried red chilies that are cut into very thin strips, and are used to garnish and add heat to many dishes. See Korean Chili Paste.

KOREAN CHILI PASTE: *Gochujang* (Korean chili paste) is available from Korean food stores, and is one of the most popular seasonings in Korean cooking. *Gochu* means chili, and *jang* refers to a salt-based flavoring sauce. *Gochujang* is made by fermenting red chili and soybean paste.

KOREAN WATERCRESS: Also known as *minari,* water dropwort, or Japanese parsley, Korean watercress is common to wetland areas and is a popular green in Korea. The taste is stronger than Western watercress.

LAVER: Known as *nori* in Japanese, laver is very thin seaweed which is edible and comes in dark brown sheets.

LEEK: Korean leek, also known as Chinese chive, resembles scallion (spring onion) and tastes similar too, without the pronounced onion flavor. Readily available from Asian markets.

LETTUCE: Use any soft-leafed lettuce for wrapping marinated meat and raw garlic.

MUSHROOMS: There are numerous varieties of mushrooms used in Korean cuisine. More commonly used varieties include *shiitake*, button, pine, winter, black, brown, and oyster mushrooms. Most of these are readily available from Asian food stores and markets in either fresh or dried form. Dried mushrooms require soaking in warm water to soften before use. If the more unusual varieties are not available (such as pine or winter), substitute with *shiitake* or button mushrooms.

NAPA CABBAGE: Also known as Korean cabbage, Chinese cabbage, and *wong nga bak*, this is the long, white cabbage and not the round variety. It is the basic ingredient of kimchi, and is also commonly used in soups. The napa cabbage is a good source of calcium, potassium, and iron.

NOODLES: Three common types of noodles used in Korea are potato or mung bean flour, buckwheat, and wheat noodles. The potato noodles are light and slippery, and are used in *japchae*; substitute these with Chinese rice vermicelli. Buckwheat noodles are usually served cold, and Japanese *soba* noodles are an acceptable substitute. The thin wheat noodles are also served cold; substitute with Japanese *somen* noodles if you can't find them in the Asian grocery.

OMIJA: These raspberry-like fruits (L. *maximowicza chinensis*) have five flavors—sweet, spicy hot, bitter, salty, and sour. It is sought for its medicinal properties, which are believed to relieve fever, thirst, and phlegm. Omija is used to make the popular omija fruit punch.

PINE NUTS: When the seeds in the pinecones ripen, the scales open and the pine nuts fall to the ground. Shelling pine nuts is difficult; one has to find a way of breaking the head black peel without marring the white kernel inside. They enrich the flavors of Korean dishes.

PERSIMMON: Fresh, ripe persimmon, with a high sugar content, and dried persimmon are both used in Korean cuisine. The dried variety is used to make a very popular Korean drink of persimmon punch.

RADISH: Also known as *mu* or *daikon*, radish appears in many different forms in Korea. Choose firm radishes and scrub well before grating or slicing.

RICE: Korean rice is a **medium grain** white rice that becomes slightly sticky when cooked, and this is the most popular variety in the Korean diet. When properly cooked, the individual grains retain their shape and do not congeal into a mass. It is not the same as **glutinous rice**, which is slightly larger. Japanese rice is very similar and makes a perfect substitute. Look for calrose rice in supermarkets. **Long grain** rice is seldom used.

RICE WINE: Also know as *makgeolli*, this very popular liquor is a low-alcohol (6 to 8 percent) beverage made by fermenting rice. A cloudy, slightly milky liquid and sometimes referred to as "farmers brew," as it was once made all over Korea by farmers, *makgeolli*, and the stronger *cheongju* rice wines, are widely available from Korean shops and make an excellent accompaniment to *anju*, or Korean snacks.

SALT: Most Koreans eat a mainly vegetarian diet, and therefore need more sodium than meat eaters. When preparing kimchi, coarse sea salt is usually used; salt is also important in the fermentation process as it provides a more complex flavor to dishes.

SCALLION: Also known as spring onion, scallion is one of many herbs used in Korean cuisine. In fact, there are many more varieties of this green onion used in Korea than are available in the West, but it is acceptable to use regular scallions as a substitute. See also Leek.

SESAME: Both sesame seeds and oil are vitally important to Korean cuisine as they are one of the most important seasonings. Black sesame seeds, used as a garnish for some dishes, are just unhulled sesame seeds.

SESAME LEAVES: These very fragrant leaves are used in a number of ways. They look similar to perilla, or Japanese shiso leaves, but the flavor is slightly different. Sesame leaves can be added to a stew at the last minute or used as a wrap.

SOY SAUCE: There are two types of soy sauces: one is the Japanese variety, which is light in color, has a distinct, salty flavor, and is used to make soups. The other type is a regular soy sauce, brownish-black in color, and not sweet. Both soy sauces are available from Asian food stores.

Radish

Sesame leaves

Omija

Dried persimmon

Part Three: The Recipes

Recipes for dips, sauces, stock, and marinades
precede those for the main dishes, which begin on page 32

Sesame Seed Dip

This delicious sesame dip is a classic accompaniment for Beef and Vegetable Hotpot (*Shinseolo*), see page 44.

> $^1/_2$ cup (45 g) sesame seeds
> $^1/_4$ cup (60 ml) light soy sauce
> 3 tablespoons rice vinegar
> 1 tablespoon sugar

Prepare sesame seed dip by toasting sesame seeds in a small pan over moderate heat, shaking frequently until golden brown. Grind or blend the seeds while still hot, adding soy sauce, vinegar, and sugar. Transfer to 4 small sauce bowls.

Soy and Vinegar Dip

Make this dip as an accompaniment for Scallion, Shellfish, and Egg Pancake (*Pa Jeon*), see page 36.

> 3 tablespoons light soy sauce
> 1 tablespoons rice vinegar
> 1 teaspoon very finely chopped garlic
> 1 teaspoon sesame oil
> 1 teaspoon sesame seeds, toasted and coarsely crushed while warm
> $^1/_4$ teaspoon freshly ground black pepper

Combine all the ingredients in a bowl and set aside.

Ingredients

When a recipe lists a hard-to-find or an unusual ingredient, see pages 24 to 27 for possible substitutes. If a substitute is not listed, look for the ingredient in your local Asian food market.

Time Estimates

Time estimates are for preparation only (excluding cooking) and are based on the assumption that a food processor or blender will be used.

🕐 *quick and very easy to prepare*

🕐🕐 *relatively easy; less than 15 minutes to prepare*

🕐🕐🕐 *takes more than 15 minutes to prepare*

Opposite:
A spread of kimchi (fermented vegetable) dishes. Clockwise from extreme left: Bossam Kimchi (Stuffed and Wrapped Vegetable Kimchi); Baek Kimchi (White Chinese Cabbage Kimchi); Nabak Kimchi (Sliced Radish and Cabbage Kimchi); Chonggak Kimchi (Bachelor Radish Kimchi), Garlic and Chives Kimchi; Leafy Green Cabbage Kimchi; and Dongchimi (Radish Water Kimchi).

Bindaettok Dipping Sauce

This simple dipping sauce is excellent with Mung Bean and Vegetable Pancake (*Bindaettok*), see page 40.

  3 tablespoons light soy sauce
  2 teaspoons rice vinegar
  1 teaspoon very finely chopped garlic
  1 teaspoon chopped scallion (spring onion)
  1 teaspoon sesame oil
  1 teaspoon toasted sesame seeds
  $1/2$ teaspoon chopped red chili
  $1/4$ teaspoon black pepper

Combine all ingredients in a bowl and mix well. Transfer to individual dipping bowls.

Daeha Naengche Sauce

A simple sauce to be poured over Cold Stuffed Tiger Prawns (*Daeha Naengche*), see page 76.

  $1/4$ cup (60 ml) rice vinegar
  1 tablespoon sugar
  1 tablespoon lemon juice
  2–3 teaspoons very finely chopped garlic
  1 teaspoon salt

Combine all the sauce ingredients shortly before serving the prawns.

Grilled Eel Sauce

This sauce is brushed over eel before and during grilling, see page 72.

  2 cloves garlic, smashed and chopped
  1 teaspoon very finely grated fresh ginger

  $1/2$ cup (125 ml) Beef Stock (see recipe on page 30)
  $1^{1}/_{2}$ tablespoons light soy sauce
  $1^{1}/_{2}$ tablespoons sugar
  1 tablespoon rice wine
  1 tablespoon sesame oil
  1 to 2 teaspoons chili powder

Combine all sauce ingredients in a small saucepan and bring to a boil. Simmer until the sauce has reduced by about half, about 10 minutes.

Mustard and Lemon Sauce

  2 teaspoons powdered mustard
  2 teaspoons sugar
  2 teaspoons vinegar
  4 teaspoons water
  Mix all ingredients thoroughly.

Bean Paste Stock

This bean paste stock is used to make Vegetables and Bean Curd Simmered in Bean Paste (*Doenjang Jjigae*), see page 60.

  4 oz (120 g) scallions (spring onions), cut in $1^{1}/_{2}$ -in (4-cm) lengths
  4 oz (120 g) salted soybean paste (yellow bean sauce)
  1–2 teaspoons chili powder
  4 tablespoons Korean chili paste (*gochujang*)
  2 cloves garlic, smashed and finely chopped
  1 teaspoon very finely grated fresh ginger
  5 oz (125 g) sirloin beef, shredded, optional
  2 heaped tablespoons dried anchovies
  3 in (8 cm) dried kelp
  $3^{1}/_{2}$ oz (100 g) long white radish, thinly sliced
  6 cups ($1^{1}/_{2}$ liters) water

Put all bean paste stock ingredients in a saucepan and bring to a boil. Lower heat, cover, and simmer 30 minutes. Pour through a sieve, discarding the solids.

Beef Stock

2 lb (1 kg) shin beef, in one piece
8 cups (2 liters) water

Put beef in a pan with water and bring to a boil. Simmer 10 minutes, then skim off all the material that has risen to the top of the liquid. Cover the pan, lower the heat and simmer very gently for 11/2 hours. Strain stock and use beef for some other purpose.

Seafood Stock

A fragrant seafood stock for use in Mixed Seafood Hotpot (*Haemul Jeongol*), see page 70.

12 mussels
6 cups (1 1/2 liters) water
3 in (8 cm) dried kelp
1 small leek, white part only, thinly sliced
6 cloves garlic, smashed and chopped
2 tablespoons Korean chili paste (*gochujang*)
1/2–1 teaspoon chili powder
1 tablespoon very finely chopped garlic
2 teaspoons very finely grated ginger
1 teaspoon salt
1 large red chili, halved lengthways
1 large green chili, halved lengthways

Make stock by combining all ingredients in a saucepan. Bring to a boil, lower heat, and simmer 15 minutes. Strain, discarding solids and reserving the stock.

Bulgogi Marinade

This marinade can be used for the meat in Skewered Pan-fried Chicken (*Dakkochi Gui*) and in Beef and Vegetable Skewers (*Sanjeok*), see both recipes on page 88.

3/4 cup (185 ml) Beef Stock (see recipe on this page)
1/3 cup (85 ml) light soy sauce
2 1/2 tablespoons sesame oil
1 1/2 tablespoon rice wine
1 1/2 tablespoon soft brown sugar
1 tablespoon very finely chopped garlic

Combine all marinade ingredients in a bowl and stir thoroughly.

Spicy Chicken Stew Marinade

This marinade is used for Spicy Chicken Stew (*Dakdoritang*) on page 84.

1/4 cup (60 ml) light soy sauce
2 tablespoons Korean chili paste (*gochujang*)
2–3 teaspoons chili powder

Combine all the marinade ingredients and stir well.

GUJEOLPAN

Nine-sectioned Royal Platter

Each person creates his or her own roll-up pancake at the table, and dips it in the sauce. ① ① ①

- $^1/_2$ cup (50 g) finely shredded canned bamboo shoot, blanched in boiling water, drained
- 1 egg, separated, lightly beaten and cooked to make 1 yellow and 1 white omelet, shredded
- 8 scallions (spring onions), cut in $1^1/_2$-in (4-cm) lengths
- 1 small canned abalone, finely julienned (optional)
- 1 small cucumber, finely julienned
- 1 small carrot, finely julienned
- 1 green bell pepper, julienned
- $^3/_4$ teaspoon sesame oil
- $^3/_4$ teaspoon salt
- Mustard and lemon sauce (see recipe on page 30)

Mushroom Filling

- 6 dried black shiitake mushrooms, soaked, liquid reserved, stems discarded, caps shredded
- 2 teaspoons light soy sauce
- $^3/_4$ teaspoon sugar
- $^1/_4$ teaspoon sesame oil

Beef Filling

- 8 oz (250 g) fillet beef, finely shredded
- 2 teaspoons light soy sauce
- $^1/_2$ teaspoon finely chopped or crushed garlic
- $^1/_2$ teaspoon sugar
- 1 teaspoon sesame oil
- 2 teaspoons vegetable oil

Pancakes

- 2 cups (250 g) all-purpose (plain) flour, sifted
- $^1/_2$ teaspoon salt
- 2 eggs, lightly beaten
- $2^1/_4$ cups (565 ml) water
- 2 teaspoons vegetable oil

Prepare the **salad fillings**. Toss the cucumber with $^1/_4$ teaspoon salt and $^1/_4$ teaspoon sesame oil. Repeat with carrot and green pepper, and place in separate dishes.

Prepare the **mushroom filling** by putting mushrooms in a small pan. Add reserved soaking liquid, soy sauce, sugar, and sesame oil. Add water to cover by $^3/_4$ in (2 cm) and simmer until soft, about 20 minutes. Transfer to a serving dish.

Prepare **beef filling** by seasoning beef with soy sauce, garlic, sugar, and sesame oil. Heat oil in a wok or large skillet, add beef, and stir-fry over high heat until just cooked. Transfer to a serving dish.

Make **pancakes** by combining flour, salt, egg, and water in a bowl. If desired, colour one-third of the batter green with lettuce juice, and one-third orange with carrot juice. Lightly oil and heat a large skillet, then pour in just enough batter to make a thin pancake. Cook, remove to a chopping board, and cut into 3-in (8-cm) circles. Repeat until all the batter is used up. Serve pancakes and all ingredients at room temperature. Serve with mustard and lemon sauce.

SONGI SANJEOK & SONGI GUI

Skewered Pine Mushrooms & Pan-fried Pine Mushrooms

SKEWERED PINE MUSHROOMS ☻

5 pine mushrooms or large forest mushrooms,
  cut in $^3/_4$-in (1-cm) slices
2–3 scallions (spring onions), cut to the same
  length as the mushrooms
2 teaspoons vegetable oil
Liberal sprinkling of salt
2 teaspoons sesame seeds

Thread the mushrooms and scallions alternately onto short bamboo skewers. Brush both sides with oil, then sprinkle salt and sesame seeds on both sides.

Cook under a hot grill, or place in a hot non-stick skillet and cook for 2 to 3 minutes on each side.

Serve warm.

PAN-FRIED PINE MUSHROOMS ☻

5 pine mushrooms, or fresh large *shiitake* or
  field mushrooms
1 teaspoon salt
2 tablespoons vegetable oil

Wipe the mushrooms with a piece of paper towel, slice into 4 or 5 pieces, then sprinkle with salt.

Heat the oil in a frying pan and add the mushrooms. Stir-fry over medium heat for 3 to 4 minutes. Serve warm.

Songi Sanjeok (Skewered Pine Mushrooms) (left); and Songi Gui (Pan-fried Pine Mushrooms) (right).

PA JEON

Scallion, Shellfish, and Egg Pancake

Pancakes are a very popular food in Korea, combining a mixture of basic ingredients in simple batter. As seafood is widely available in most of the country, pancakes containing oysters or mixed seafood are often found. Plenty of chopped scallions add extra flavour to this version, which contains oysters. ☮

1/3 cup (40 g) glutinous rice flour or cornflour
1/3 cup (40 g) rice flour
1/3 cup (40 g) all-purpose (plain) flour
1 egg, lightly beaten
1 teaspoon salt
Liberal sprinkling white pepper
3/4 cup (185 ml) water
3–4 scallions (spring onions), cut in 1 1/4-in (3-cm) lengths (some green stems left whole)
1/2 cup (100 g) fresh oysters, rinsed and drained
Generous pinch of dried chili strips, or 1 red chili, finely julienned
1/4 cup (60 ml) vegetable oil
1 portion Soy and Vinegar Dip (see recipe on page 29)

Combine the flours, egg, salt, and pepper, stirring in water to make a smooth, reasonably thin batter. Stir in the scallions, oysters, and chili, and set aside.

Heat 2 tablespoons of the oil in a skillet and, when moderately hot, add a small ladleful of batter, spreading to make a thin pancake about 4 in (10 cm) across. Cook until golden brown underneath and starting to set on top, about 2 minutes, then turn over and cook until light brown on the other side. Repeat until all the mixture is used up.

Serve hot with the **Soy and Vinegar Dip.**

Helpful hint: To save time, you could make 1 large pancake and cut it in to serving pieces, rather than prepare small pancakes. If desired, the oysters can be omitted and the amount of scallions doubled to make a Scallion Pancake.

MILSSAM

Traditional Pancake Rolls

Prepare these rolls with a tasty filling of beef, vegetables, and omelet before bringing them to the table. Alternatively, for a more informal gathering, put everything on the table and let all diners help themselves. ☻ ☻

1½ tablespoons sesame oil
6½ oz (200 g) beef, shredded
1 slender Asian cucumber, finely julienned
4 dried black mushrooms, soaked and shredded
1 medium green chili, finely julienned
1 small carrot, finely julienned
3 oz (80 g) finely shredded canned
   bamboo shoot
1 teaspoon salt
4 eggs, separated
2 teaspoons vegetable oil
3 tablespoons pine nuts, crushed
Mustard and lemon sauce (optional, see recipe
   on page 30)

Batter
2 cups (320 g) rice flour
1 teaspoon salt
2 cups (500 ml) water

Prepare the **batter** by combining all ingredients to make a very thin batter. If desired, colour one-third of the batter green with lettuce juice, and one-third orange with carrot juice. Lightly grease the bottom of a small skillet, about 6 in (15 cm) in diameter, and heat. Add about 2 tablespoons of the rice-flour batter and swirl the pan immediately to cover the bottom. Cook over medium heat until set, then turn and cook the other side. Repeat until the batter is used up.

Sprinkle beef, cucumber, mushrooms, green chili, carrot, and bamboo shoot with a little salt and the sesame oil. Set aside.

Lightly beat egg yolks with 1 teaspoon water. Beat the egg whites separately. Grease a skillet with a little oil, heat, then fry the beaten yolks to make thin omelets. Transfer to a plate. Repeat with the egg white. Shred both omelets finely and set aside.

Heat 2 teaspoons oil in a wok or skillet and stir-fry the beef until just cooked. Transfer to a plate. Add another 2 teaspoons oil and stir-fry the cucumber for just 1 minute. Repeat for the mushrooms, green chili, and bamboo shoot, heating 2 teaspoons oil before adding each separately to the wok and stir-frying just until each vegetable is cooked.

Put a little of the omelet, beef, and vegetables into a rice-flour pancake and roll up, tucking in the sides. Sprinkle with crushed pine nuts to garnish and serve at room temperature. If preferred, serve the rice wrappers and filling ingredients separately, with the pine nuts for garnishing. Dip into the mustard and lemon sauce if desired.

BINDAETTOK & MODEUM JEON

Mung Bean and Vegetable Pancake & Pan-fried Beef, Fish, and Zucchini

Soaked and ground mung beans add extra texture and flavor to these pancakes, which also contain crunchy bean sprouts and shredded cabbage. This recipe makes enough for 4 when the pancakes are served as a starter, or as part of any meal with rice and other dishes. You'll need to start 4 hours in advance to soak the mung beans, but the final preparation is quick and easy. ✆

Bindaettok
(Mung Bean and Vegetable Pancake) (left); and Modeum Jeon (Pan-fried, Beef, Fish, and Zucchini) (right). For recipe of Modeum Jeon, see page 118.

$^1/_4$ cup (50 g) skinned mung beans, soaked 4 hours, drained
3 eggs
1 cup (80 g) mung bean sprouts, straggly tails removed
$^1/_4$ cup (20 g) kimchi, rinsed
1 tablespoon very finely chopped onion
1 scallion (spring onion), cut in $^3/_4$-in (2-cm) lengths
$^1/_2$ cup (40–50 g) chopped fern tips, optional
1 teaspoon finely grated fresh ginger
1 teaspoon sesame oil
1 teaspoon salt
Liberal sprinkling white pepper
1 tablespoon all-purpose (plain) flour
1 tablespoon rice flour
2 tablespoons vegetable oil
1 portion Bindaettok Dipping Sauce (see recipe on page 30)

Put the mung beans in a food processor and blend until ground, adding up to 3 tablespoons water to produce a slightly coarse paste. The ground beans can be refrigerated in a covered container for several hours.

Put eggs in a bowl and beat lightly. Stir in ground mung beans, mixing well, then add bean sprouts, kimchi, onion, scallion, fern tips, ginger, sesame, salt, and pepper, tossing gently. Add both lots of flour and toss again.

Heat 2 to 3 teaspoons oil in a skillet and add spoonfuls of the mixture to make several pancakes about 3 in (8 cm) in diameter. Cook over medium heat until brown underneath, 2 to 3 minutes, then turn and cook the other side. Drain on paper towel and keep warm. Repeat until mixture is used up.

Serve the pancakes with the **Bindaettok Dipping Sauce**.

Helpful hint: If skinned mung beans, which are split and pale yellow in color, are not available, use whole green mung beans, which must be soaked for 2 days before the skin can be slipped off.

JAOTJUK & HOBAKJUK & JEONBOKJUK

Pine Nut Porridge & Pumpkin Porridge & Abalone Porridge

PINE NUT PORRIDGE

1 cup (200 g) rice, soaked in plenty of water
   for 4 hours, drained
1 cup (150 g) pine nuts
5 cups (1¼ liters) water
1 teaspoon salt

Combine drained rice, pine nuts, and 2 cups of the water in a blender. Blend until coarsely ground, but do not blend so long that it forms a paste.

Put blended rice mixture into a deep saucepan. Add remaining 3 cups of water, bring to a boil over medium heat, stirring constantly. Lower heat and simmer uncovered, stirring several times, until the porridge is thick and well cooked, about 25 minutes. Stir in salt and serve.

PUMPKIN PORRIDGE

1 lb (500 g) peeled pumpkin, cut in ½-in
   (1-cm) dice
5 cups (1¼ liters) water
⅓ cup (50 g) rice flour
1 tablespoon soft brown sugar
1 teaspoon salt
2 tablespoons toasted pumpkin seeds (pepitas)

Put the pumpkin in a saucepan with 4 cups (1 liter) of the water. Bring to a boil, cover, and simmer until the pumpkin is very soft and breaks up completely when stirred with a wooden spoon, about 25 minutes.

Mix the rice flour with the remaining cup of water, then stir in to the pumpkin mixture. Bring to a boil over medium heat, stirring constantly. Lower heat and simmer 2 minutes. Stir in the sugar and salt, then divide between 4 serving bowls, topping each serving with some of the pumpkin seeds. (Note: Different varieties of pumpkin may be used.)

ABALONE PORRIDGE

2 teaspoons sesame oil
1 cup (200 g) rice, soaked in plenty of water
   for 4 hours, drained
5 cups (1¼ liters) water
1 teaspoon salt
4 oz (125 g) canned abalone, thinly sliced and
   patted dry
4 egg yolks (optional)

Heat the sesame oil in a deep saucepan and fry the drained rice to coat well. Add water and bring to a boil over medium heat, stirring frequently. Lower heat and simmer with the pan partially covered with the lid, stirring several times, until the rice is very tender, 30 to 45minutes. Add the abalone slices and salt and heat through. Serve in 4 bowls, with a raw egg yolk served separately in a small bowl if desired.

APPETIZERS

SHINSEOLO

Beef and Vegetable Hotpot

1 medium carrot, julienned
$\frac{1}{2}$ cup (60 g) all-purpose (plain) flour
$3\frac{1}{2}$ oz (100 g) firm bean curd, julienned
6–8 g fresh *shiitake* or brown mushrooms,
   thickly sliced
1 cup (250 ml) vegetable oil
1 egg, lightly beaten
8 oz (250 g) beef fillet or sirloin, very
   thinly sliced
1 small long white radish, thinly sliced
2 cloves garlic, smashed and finely chopped
1 teaspoon sesame oil
1 tablespoon pine nuts
8 dried chestnuts, soaked in warm water
   30 minutes, simmered until soft
4 cups (1 liter) beef stock (see recipe on page 30)
Salt to taste
Liberal grinding black pepper
1 portion Sesame Seed Dip (optional)
   (see recipe on page 29)

Optional items

8 oz (250 g) liver, dipped in flour and egg and
   fried until just cooked before adding to pot
8 oz (250 g) white fish fillet, prepared as for
   the liver
20–25 ginkgo nuts
Meatballs (marinate minced meat with pepper,
   garlic, sesame oil, and salt, and then roll in
   flour and egg, and pan-fry 5 minutes)
Steamed shrimps
Red chilies, cut in rectangles

Prepare **Sesame Seed Dip** if using .

Toss carrot in flour and shake off excess. Repeat for soybean curd and mushrooms and set aside. Heat oil in a wok and when very hot, dip the carrot in egg, add to wok and stir-fry until golden brown. Remove and drain on paper towel. Repeat for the bean curd and mushrooms, dipping each in flour and egg and deep-frying.

Put the beef and radish in the moat of a steamboat pot or firekettle and sprinkle with the garlic and sesame oil. Spread the fried ingredients over, then add pine nuts, chestnuts and any optional items. (At this stage, the food can be covered and kept for 1 to 2 hours before finalizing the dish.)

Bring beef stock to a boil, then carefully pour into the moat to cover the ingredients. Taste and add salt if desired, then sprinkle with pepper. Cover the moat and add glowing red coals to the central chimney and allow the contents to simmer for a few minutes. Each person may then help themselves to the contents with chopsticks. When all the meat and vegetables are finished, spoon the soup into small bowls and enjoy.

Helpful hint: If you do not have a steamboat pot, place a fondue or casserole on a table-top cooker.

NAMUL

Trio of Vegetables

Side-dishes of several types of simmered and seasoned vegetable are almost invariably served as part of a main meal in Korea. Leafy greens, mushrooms, eggplant, long white radish, bellflower root, cucumber, and bean sprouts can all be prepared in this fashion, delicately seasoned and prepared with a minimum of oil. ☯ ☯

- 1 lb (500 g) spinach, washed and drained, blanched in boiling water 30 seconds, chopped
- ³/₄ cup (185 ml) water
- 3 teaspoons sesame oil
- 2 teaspoons sesame seeds, toasted and coarsely crushed while still warm
- ¹/₂ teaspoon salt
- 8 oz (250 g) fresh bellflower root, washed and drained, blanched in boiling water 30 seconds, chopped, or cucumber, chopped
- 8 fresh *shiitake* mushrooms or brown mushrooms, stems discarded, caps sliced
- 1 tablespoon soy sauce
- 2 tablespoons rice wine
- 2 teaspoons sugar

Put spinach in a saucepan and add 2 tablespoons water and 1 teaspoon sesame oil, 1 teaspoon sesame seeds, and ¹/₄ teaspoon salt. Cover, bring to a boil, lower heat, and simmer until the spinach is tender, 3 to 4 minutes. Transfer to a serving dish.

Repeat for bellflower root or cucumber, cooking it with 2 tablespoons water and 1 teaspoon sesame oil, 1 teaspoon sesame seeds, and ¹/₄ teaspoon salt. Arrange on the same serving dish as the spinach.

Put mushrooms in a small saucepan and add remaining ¹/₂ cup (125 ml) water, 1 teaspoon sesame oil, the soy sauce, rice wine, and sugar. Bring to a boil, cover, and simmer until the mushrooms are cooked, about 5 minutes. Place the mushrooms decoratively beside the other vegetables and serve warm or at room temperature.

MYULCHI BOKEUM & SOGOGI JANGCHORIM

Fried Anchovies & Beef Casserole

FRIED ANCHOVIES

3 oz (80 g) dried cleaned anchovies (about
    2 in or 5 cm in length), or $3^1/_2$ oz (100 g)
    whole dried baby anchovies
2 in (5 cm) ginger
2 teaspoons water
3 tablespoons vegetable oil
2 teaspoons very finely chopped garlic
2 teaspoons sugar
$^1/_2$–1 teaspoon crushed dried chili (optional)
1 teaspoon sesame oil
1 teaspoon toasted sesame seeds, for garnishing

If anchovies are not purchased cleaned, discard the heads and the dark intestinal tract. Do not wash the anchovies.

Put the ginger and water in a spice grinder and blend. Put in a sieve and press down to obtain 1 teaspoon ginger juice. Set aside.

Heat the oil in a wok and add the anchovies. Stir-fry over medium heat until crisp and cooked, 5 minutes. Remove anchovies from wok and drain on paper towel. Clean the wok and return to the heat. Add anchovies and sprinkle with ginger juice, garlic, and sugar and stir-fry 1 minute. Add chili and sesame oil and stir-fry for a few seconds, then mix well. Transfer to a serving dish, garnish with toasted sesame seeds, and serve at room temperature.

BEEF CASSEROLE

This simple recipe needs almost no preparation, although it does take some time to cook. While waiting for the meat to cook, you can prepare rice and a vegetable dish or two to accompany the beef, and perhaps serve a side-dish of kimchi. ⏱

$1^1/_2$–2 lb ($^3/_4$–1 kg) meaty beef, cut in bite-
    sized pieces
$^2/_3$ oz (20 g) onion
$^2/_3$ oz (20 g) dried red pepper
$6^1/_2$ oz (200 g) leek, cut in large pieces
$6^1/_2$ oz (200 g) garlic cloves, peeled
1 cup (250 ml) water
85 ml ($^1/_3$ cup) light soy sauce
1 teaspoon sugar
1 teaspoon very finely chopped garlic
6 hard-boiled quail eggs

Put beef in a saucepan and cover with water. Bring to a boil, cover, lower heat and simmer until meat is just tender. Drain, keeping stock aside for some other dish, then return meat to the pan with all the remaining ingredients except the eggs. Bring to a boil, cover and simmer for 30 to 45 minutes, stirring from time to time, until the beef is very tender. Serve with quail eggs and steamed rice.

YANGNYEUMJANG SUNDUBU

Bean Curd with Spicy Sauce

A delicious and spicy way of serving bean curd. ①

10 oz (300 g) soft bean curd, chilled and cut in 4 pieces or left whole

Sauce

4 teaspoons light soy sauce
1 teaspoon sesame seeds, toasted and lightly crushed while warm
1 teaspoon sesame oil
1 clove garlic, smashed and very finely chopped
1 teaspoon chili powder
1 teaspoon water
1 teaspoon very finely chopped scallion (spring onion)
1 fresh chili, finely chopped (optional)
A generous pinch of dried red chili strips, for garnishing

Put a piece of bean curd on each of 4 small bowls (or the whole bean curd on one serving bowl).

Combine all **sauce** ingredients, stirring to mix well, then drizzle the sauce over the top of each serving of bean curd. Garnish with finely chopped fresh chili and a generous pinch of dried red chili strips, if desired.

Serve as a side dish with rice and other dishes.

KIMCHI

Whole Cabbage Kimchi

This popular type of kimchi or fermented pickle uses long white Chinese cabbage mixed with shredded long white radish, scallion, and leek and is seasoned with chili, garlic, and ginger. This kimchi should be refrigerated once the fermentation process has been completed. ☻ ☻

- 1 long white napa (Chinese) cabbage, about 1 lb 3 oz (600 g)
- $\frac{1}{2}$ cup (125 g) coarse or pickling salt
- 4 cups (1 liter) water
- 1 small long white radish, about 5 oz (160 g), cut in $1\frac{1}{2}$-in (4-cm) julienne strips
- 1 scallion (spring onion), cut in $1\frac{1}{2}$-in (4-cm) julienne strips
- 1 small leek, white part only, cut in $1\frac{1}{2}$-in (4-cm) julienne strips
- 2 teaspoons very finely chopped garlic
- 1 teaspoon finely grated ginger
- $1\frac{1}{2}$–2 tablespoons chili powder
- 1 teaspoon sugar
- $\frac{1}{6}$ oz (5 g) pickled shrimp
- $\frac{2}{3}$ oz (20 g) salted anchovies

Trim off the root end of the cabbage but do not cut or separate the leaves. Put all but $1\frac{1}{2}$ tablespoons of the salt in a large bowl and add 4 cups (1 liter) water. Stir to dissolve, then add cabbage, bending the end if necessary to fit the cabbage in tightly. Add more water if needed to cover. Put a weighted plate on top to keep the cabbage under the salted water, and keep at room temperature for 12 hours or longer if needed until the cabbage has softened. Drain the cabbage, rinse well under running water, and squeeze dry.

Combine all other ingredients in a bowl, tossing to mix well. Stand the cabbage upright in a bowl and separate the leaves, one by one, pushing in some of the radish mixture by hand to fill. Pack the cabbage, pushing it down firmly into a covered jar just large enough to hold it. Press down to remove any pockets of air, then cover the jar.

Refrigerate 2 hours, then transfer jar to a warm place—around 78°F (25°C) for about 24 hours to ferment. Transfer to a fridge and chill. Chop before serving.

Helpful hint: Never use a reactive metal container to store kimchi; use porcelain or stainless steel. Plastic will be permanently stained by chili. Store kimchi in a cool, dark place—a fridge is best.

MUL KIMCHI & OISOBAEGI

Water Kimchi & Stuffed Cucumber Kimchi

Although this dish is classified as kimchi, due to the large amount of water, it is more like a soup. ◷ ◷

13 oz (400 g) long white napa (Chinese) cabbage, each leaf cut in 1-in (2$\frac{1}{2}$-cm) squares
6$\frac{1}{2}$ oz (200 g) long white radish, thinly sliced
2 tablespoons plus 2 teaspoons salt
2 in (5 cm) fresh ginger, chopped
4 cloves garlic, chopped
2 teaspoons sugar
1–2 teaspoons chili powder

Garnish

Sprigs of fresh cilantro (coriander)
2 tablespoons chopped scallion (spring onion)
1 small slender cucumber, sliced
$\frac{1}{4}$ Asian pear (*nashi*), peeled and sliced

Mul Kimchi (Water Kimchi) (left) and Oisobaegi (Stuffed Cucumber Kimchi) (right). Recipe for Oisobaegi is on page 118.

Put cut cabbage and radish in a large bowl and add 2 tablespoons salt. Massage with the hands for 1 minute, then cover loosely and leave to stand 2 hours. Put vegetables in a sieve above a bowl and squeeze, keeping the salty water. Rinse the vegetables under running water, drain, and squeeze. Put vegetables in a jar, pressing down well to get rid of any pockets of air. Combine the reserved salty water with fresh water to make 2 cups.

Process 2 teaspoons salt, ginger, and garlic in a spice grinder, adding a little water if needed to get a paste. Add this paste, the sugar, and chili powder to the reserved water, stirring to dissolve, then pour over the vegetables. Cover the jar with plastic wrap and keep in a warm place for 2 to 3 days to allow to ferment, then refrigerate.

To serve, put some the cabbage, radish, and the pickling water in a bowl, garnish with cilantro, scallion, cucumber, and pear and serve with rice and other dishes.

DUBU KIMCHI

Bean Curd Kimchi

This is a very quick and easy dish, ideal for a simple meal with rice and perhaps a bowl of light soup. Sliced beef is quickly stir-fried with ready made kimchi, with scallions, and garlic to taste; bean curd is added at the last minute for a flavorful and nutritious meal. ✆

1 tablespoon vegetable oil
2 teaspoons sesame oil
6½ oz (200 g) beef fillet or sirloin, or belly of pork, thinly sliced
1–2 teaspoons finely chopped garlic
1 red chili, sliced (optional)
1–2 scallions (spring onions), cut in ¾-in (2-cm) lengths
1 lb (500 g) kimchi, drained and coarsely chopped
10 oz (300 g) bean curd, cut in bite-sized pieces
½ teaspoon toasted black sesame seeds, for garnishing

Heat both lots of oil in a wok and stir-fry beef over high heat until it changes color. Add the garlic, chili, and spring onions and stir-fry for a few seconds, then add kimchi and stir-fry until it is thoroughly heated, about 1 minute. Transfer to a serving dish and keep warm.

Put the tofu pieces in a colander or sieve and carefully lower into boiling water. Leave for 30 seconds to heat through (longer if using directly from the fridge), then drain and carefully transfer to one side of the serving plate. Garnish with the toasted black sesame seeds, and serve immediately with rice.

KIMCHI JJIGAE

Kimchi Stew

The liberal amount of chili in this satisfying soup (in both the prepared kimchi and in the form of extra chili powder) means that it is very good for clearing nasal passages and is therefore regarded as a remedy for cold symptoms in Korea. Even if you don't have a cold, you can enjoy this tangy dish, halfway between a soup and a stew, with plenty of neutralizing steamed white rice. ☻

1 tablespoon vegetable oil
4 oz (120 g) beef sirloin, finely shredded
1–2 teaspoons smashed and very finely
    chopped garlic
2¼ cups firmly packed (480 g) sliced kimchi
6 cups (1½ liters) Beef Stock (see recipe on
    page 31)
4 oz (120 g) bean curd, sliced into rectangles
    about 1¼ by 1 in (3 cm by 2 cm)
1–2 teaspoons chili powder
2 scallions (spring onions), thinly sliced
1 small red or green chili, sliced

Heat the oil in a cast iron pot and stir-fry the beef until it changes color. Add the garlic and kimchi and stir-fry for a couple of minutes, then add the **Beef Stock**. Bring to a boil and simmer 1 minute. Add the bean curd and chili powder, return to a boil, and simmer 2 minutes. Sprinkle with scallions and sliced chilies, and serve hot.

Helpful hint: The beef can be replaced by pork. Some cooks like to substitute about 1 cup (250 ml) of the beef stock with juice drained from the kimchi jar.

DOENJANG JJIGAE

Vegetables and Bean Curd Simmered in Bean Paste

1 portion Bean Paste Stock (see recipe on
  page 30)
4 oz (120 g) sirloin beef, shredded
5 oz (125 g) peeled pumpkin (winter squash),
  cut in ³/₄-in (1¹/₂-cm) pieces
1 small red or green bell pepper (capsicum),
  cut in ³/₄-in (1¹/₂-cm) pieces
5 oz (125 g) bean curd, cut in ³/₄-in
  (1¹/₂-cm) cubes
2–3 dried *shiitake* mushrooms, soaked in water
  to soften, stems discarded, caps quartered
1 large red chili, seeded and sliced
1 large green chili, seeded and sliced
8 small clams (optional)
4 small abalone (optional)
2 scallions (spring onion), thinly sliced,
  for garnishing

Prepare the **Bean Paste Stock**. After sieving the stock and discarding the solids, return the sieved stock to the saucepan and add the beef, vegetables, and bean curd.

Bring to a boil, reduce heat, and simmer until the vegetables are cooked. Add the clams and abalone, if using, and simmer until they open. Serve with rice.

Helpful hint: For a more substantial meal if not serving other dishes with the rice, double the amount of pumpkin, bell pepper, bean curd, beef, and mushroom.

YUKGAEJANG

Spicy Beef Soup

This tangy, piping hot soup is a favourite on hot summer days in Korea. This may seem strange, but the liberal amount of chili encourages perspiration, thus cooling the body. Even if you serve this in the middle of winter, you'll find it a robust soup ideal with rice. ◷

1 lb (500 g) flank or shin beef, in one piece
6 cups (1¹/₂ liters) water
1 teaspoon salt
6¹/₂ oz (200 g) mung bean sprouts, straggly tails removed
8–10 scallions (spring onions), cut in 1¹/₄-in (3-cm) lengths
5 teaspoons light soy sauce
1 tablespoon smashed and finely chopped garlic
4 teaspoons chili powder
4 teaspoons Korean chili paste (*gochujang*)
1 teaspoon sesame oil
2 eggs

Put beef in a saucepan with the water and salt. Bring to a boil, cover, lower heat, and simmer until the beef is tender. Remove beef and shred very finely.

Return beef to the stock and add bean sprouts and scallions. Bring to a boil and simmer 5 minutes. Add soy sauce, garlic, chili powder, chili paste, and sesame oil, and simmer for a few seconds. Just before serving, stir in the eggs gently.

BUKOH CONGNAMUL GUK

Dried Pollack Soup with Bean Sprouts

2 oz (50 g) dried pollack or other dried cod, soaked in water 20 to 30 minutes, then thinly sliced

1 lb (500 g) bean sprouts

Salt to taste

Liberal sprinkling white pepper

1 egg

1 tablespoon seeded large red chili, thinly sliced

1 tablespoon seeded large green chili, thinly sliced

Chili powder

Stock

$3^{1}/_{2}$ oz (100 g) long white radish, thinly sliced

$3^{1}/_{2}$ oz (100 g) leeks, thinly sliced

3 in (8 cm) dried kelp

$^{3}/_{4}$ in (2 cm) piece fresh ginger, thinly sliced

6 cloves garlic, smashed

6 cups ($1^{1}/_{2}$ liters) water

To prepare the **stock**, put all ingredients into a large saucepan. Bring to a boil, cover, and simmer 10 minutes. Strain stock and discard the solids.

Put the stock back in the pan and bring to a boil. Add the fish and simmer 3 minutes. Add the bean sprouts and simmer 2 minutes. Add salt to taste, sprinkle with pepper, and transfer to a serving bowl. Add the egg.

Garnish with the sliced chilies, and serve chili powder in a side dish.

SUNDUBU JJIGAE

Soft Bean Curd Soup with Beef

1 tablespoon vegetable oil
2 teaspoons sesame oil
4 oz (120 g) beef fillet or sirloin, thinly sliced
1–2 teaspoons finely chopped garlic
1–2 scallions (spring onions), cut in $^3/_4$-in
  (2-cm) lengths
1 lb (500 g) kimchi, drained and coarsely
  chopped
6 cups (1$^1/_2$ liters) water
$^1/_2$ oz (15 g) salted anchovies
3 in (8 cm) dried kelp
8–12 small clams
10 oz (300 g) bean curd, cut in bite-sized
  pieces

Heat both lots of oil in a saucepan and stir-fry beef over high heat until it changes color. Add the garlic and scallions and stir-fry for a few seconds. Then, add kimchi and stir-fry until it is thoroughly heated, about 1 minute.

Add the water, anchovies, and kelp. Bring to a boil, then switch off heat, and add clams and bean curd. Leave for 30 seconds to heat through (longer if using bean curd pieces directly from the fridge).

Serve immediately with rice, kimchi, and a side dish of your choice.

SOGOGI DUBU JEONGOL & BEOSOT JEONGOL

Stuffed Bean Curd and Beef Casserole & Mushroom Casserole

STUFFED BEAN CURD AND BEEF CASSEROLE

6$^{1}/_{2}$ in (200 g) finely minced lean beef
$^{1}/_{2}$ teaspoon sesame oil
$^{1}/_{2}$ teaspoon smashed and finely chopped garlic
$^{1}/_{4}$ teaspoon salt
Freshly ground black pepper
$^{1}/_{4}$ cup (60 ml) vegetable oil
4 pieces bean curd, about 5 oz (150 g) each
6$^{1}/_{2}$ in (200 g) beef sirloin, cut in 8 thin slices
1 bunch fresh cilantro (coriander), stems
  separated, or 8 scallions (spring onions),
  blanched briefly to soften
2 red bell peppers (capsicum), sliced
6 cups (1$^{1}/_{2}$ liters) beef stock
1 egg yolk, lightly beaten
A generous pinch of chili powder

Put the minced beef in a small bowl and add sesame oil, garlic, salt and pepper. Mix well and set aside.

Cut each piece of bean curd in half horizontally—it should be about $^{3}/_{4}$ in (2 cm) thick after cutting. Place on paper towel and pat dry. Heat the oil, then fry the bean curd until golden brown on both sides, turning carefully. Drain on paper towel. When cool, cut each piece in half horizontally.

Divide the minced beef into 8 portions and flatten with the hands to the same size as the bean curd. Place a beef portion onto a piece of bean curd and

top with a second piece of bean curd. Tie each bean curd "sandwich" with a stem of fresh cilantro or the green portion of a scallion. Arrange the stuffed bean curd in casserole, add the sirloin, bell pepper, and a sprinkling of chili powder. Pour in beef stock, bring to a boil, cover and simmer gently for 10 minutes. Pour over the egg yolk and serve hot.

MUSHROOM CASSEROLE

1$^{1}/_{2}$ lb (750 g) mixed fresh mushrooms
  (*shiitake*, brown mushrooms, oyster
  mushrooms, and button mushrooms)
3 oz (80 g) long white napa (Chinese) cabbage,
  cut in 2-in (5-cm) lengths
4–6 scallions (spring onions), cut in 2-in
  (5-cm) lengths, some stems left whole
$^{1}/_{2}$ red bell pepper (capsicum), cut in strips
10 oz (300 g) beef sirloin, thinly sliced
6 cups (1$^{1}/_{2}$ liters) beef stock
Salt and black pepper to taste

Discard the tough mushroom stems, and cut caps into strips. Arrange all ingredients except the beef stock in a heat-proof casserole. Bring the beef stock to a boil, then add to the casserole. Bring to a boil slowly, then simmer until the mushrooms are cooked, about 10 minutes. Taste the soup and add salt if desired. Sprinkle with black pepper and serve hot with rice.

HAEMUL JEONGOL

Mixed Seafood Hotpot

This spicy mixture of seafood is generally served in the pan in which it is cooked, with everyone helping themselves to morsels of crab, octopus, prawn, clam, and mussel, together with some of the rich stock. This is best accompanied by a bowl of steamed white rice, and finger bowls for use after handling the crab. ① ①

1 portion Seafood Stock (see recipe on page 31)
2 red chilies, seeded and sliced
2 green chilies, seeded and sliced
1 large blue swimmer crab, cleaned and cut in 4 pieces, legs cracked
10 oz (300 g) octopus or squid, cut in 2-in (5-cm) pieces
4 tiger prawns or 8 medium raw prawns, peeled and deveined
8–12 small clams, scrubbed with a brush and soaked in salty water 20 minutes
2 medium-sized abalone
4 oz (125 g) long white napa (Chinese) cabbage, cut in 2-in (5-cm) lengths
1 piece bean curd, about 5 oz (150 g), cut in $3/4$-in (2-cm) dice
2 tablespoons chopped fresh cilantro (coriander)
2 scallions (spring onions), thinly sliced
Fresh crown daisy, for garnishing
A generous pinch of dried chili powder

Prepare the **Seafood Stock.** Strain the stock and discard the solids.

Arrange the crab, octopus, prawns, clams, abalone, cabbage, and bean curd in a wide casserole. Carefully pour in the stock around the edge of the pan, bring to a boil, cover, and simmer until cooked, about 10 to 15 minutes. Then add the cilantro and scallions.

Garnish with crown daisy and sprinkle with chili powder. Serve with steamed rice.

JANGEO GUI & EUNDAEGU GANJANG GUI & OKDOM GUI

Grilled Eel & Grilled Cod & Grilled Red Snapper

Left to right:
Okdom Gui
(Grilled Red
Snapper),
Jangeo Gui
(Grilled Eel),
and Eundaegu
Ganjang Gui
(Grilled Cod).
For recipe of
Okdom Gui
(Grilled Red
Snapper), see
page 74.

GRILLED EEL

1 fresh eel, weighing about 2 lb (1 kg), filleted
1 portion Grilled Eel Sauce (see recipe on
   page 30)
1 tablespoon sesame seeds, toasted and
   coarsely crushed while still warm
1 tablespoon finely chopped scallion
   (spring onion)
Liberal sprinkling of white pepper
Very finely grated ginger and sliced grilled
   garlic to garnish

To hold eel fillets straight during cooking, skewer fillets lengthways, with 2 bamboo skewers in each fillet. Prepare the **Grilled Eel Sauce** and simmer until the sauce has reduced by half, about 10 minutes. Brush a griller or table-top grill lightly with oil. Heat until very hot, then put on eel fillets, skin side away from heat, and grill 3 minutes. Turn and grill other side for 3 minutes.

Brush one side of the eel with sauce and grill 1 minute. Turn, brush other side, and grill 1 minute. Repeat twice. Cut eel into $2^{1}/_{2}$-in (6-cm) pieces and put on 4 serving dishes. Sprinkle with sesame seeds, scallion, and pepper and serve hot garnished with the ginger and grilled garlic.

GRILLED COD

1 lb 3 oz (600 g) cod or other white fish fillets,
   in 4 pieces
Slices of lemon to garnish

Marinade
$^{1}/_{2}$ cup (125 ml) water
3 tablespoons light soy sauce
1 tablespoons sugar
1 tablespoon rice wine
2 teaspoons lime or lemon juice
$^{1}/_{2}$ teaspoon sesame oil

Put the fish fillets in a wide bowl. Combine all the marinade ingredients and pour over the fish. Leave to stand for about 5 minutes. Drain fish and put the marinade ingredients into a small saucepan. Bring to the boil, then keep warm.

Cook the fish under a hot grill until cooked, about 3 to 4 minutes on either side, depending on the thickness of the fish. Transfer to a serving dish and spoon over a little of the hot sauce. Garnish with lemon and serve hot.

URUKMAEUNTANG & OKDOM GUI

Black Rock Fish Soup & Grilled Red Snapper

BLACK ROCK FISH SOUP ⏱

4 cups (1 liter) water
2–3 teaspooons chili powder
4 cloves garlic, smashed and finely chopped
2 teaspoons finely grated fresh ginger
1 teaspoon salt
2 oz (60 g) long white radish, cut in $^3/_4$-in
   ($1^1/_2$-cm) dice
2 oz (60 g) pumpkin, cut in half moon wedges
2 oz (60 g) leek, thinly sliced
$^1/_2$ small onion, thinly sliced
2 lb (1 kg) black rock fish or other white fish,
   cut in steaks or cutlets
5 oz (125 g) bean curd, cut in $^3/_4$-in
   ($1^1/_2$-cm) dice
$^1/_4$ cup coarsely chopped fresh cilantro
   (coriander) leaves
1 large red chili, sliced
1 large green chili, sliced
$1^1/_3$ oz (40 g) scallion (spring onion), sliced
Liberal sprinkling white pepper
Crown daisies to garnish, optional

Put the water, chili powder, garlic, ginger, and
salt in a large saucepan and bring to a boil. Add
radish, pumpkin, leek, and onion and simmer
5 minutes. Add the fish and cook 5 minutes, then
put in the bean curd, coriander leaf, and chilies
and simmer uncovered until the fish is tender.
Sprinkle with scallions and white pepper and, if
desired, decorate with a crown daisy.

GRILLED RED SNAPPER

The photograph of Grilled Red Snapper appears on
page 72. ⏱

1 fresh red snapper fillet or other white-fleshed
   fish fillet, about $1^1/_2$ oz (750 g)
1 tablespoon salt
2–3 teaspoons sesame oil
Lemon slices to garnish
Sprigs of parsley to garnish

Wash and dry the fillet, then sprinkle salt over both
sides. Stand in the fridge for 30 minutes, then rinse
fillet briefly, and pat dry with paper towel. Paint
both sides of the fish generously with sesame oil,
then cook under a hot grill or over charcoal until
done. Transfer to a serving dish and garnish with
lemon and parsley.

DAEHA NAENGCHE

Cold Stuffed Tiger Prawns

This excellent appetizer of prawns filled with crunchy, refreshing strips of pear and cucumber and served with a tangy vinegar-garlic dressing is best made with large tiger prawns, about 5 oz (150 g) each. The jelly fish strips used to secure the filling add a delicious crunchy texture, although if it is more convenient, blanched scallions could be used instead. ✆

   4 raw large tiger prawns, washed and drained
   1¹/₂–2 cups (375–500 ml) water
   1 scallion (spring onion), chopped
   ¹/₂ small onion, thinly sliced
   4 slices lemon
   1 portion Daeha Naengche Sauce (see recipe
      on page 30)
   3-in (8-cm) piece cucumber, finely
      julienned
   ¹/₂ Asian pear (*nashi*), finely julienned
   2 oz (50 g) jelly fish, blanched in boiling water
      to soften, cut in 4 narrow strips
      8 in (20 cm) long, or 4 scallions (spring
      onions), trimmed 8 in (20 cm) in length
      and blanched to soften

Skewer each prawn lengthwise with a bamboo skewer, from the tail end through to the head, to hold the prawn straight during cooking. Put sufficient water to cover the prawns in a wide saucepan and add scallion, onion, and lemon slices. Bring to a boil, lower heat and simmer 2 minutes then add the prawns. Cook until they turn red and are cooked through, about 4 minutes. Drain prawns and leave to cool; they can be refrigerated in a covered container for several hours if liked.

Shortly before serving, prepare **Daeha Naenghe Sauce** and set aside. Remove skewers from the prawns, peel but leave the heads and tails intact. Cut a slash down the back of each prawn and remove any dark vein. Place strips of cucumber and pear on the underside of the prawns, press together by hand, then tie each prawn with a roll of jelly fish strips. Put each prawn on a small plate, pour the sauce over and serve.

DAEHAP JJIM & DAEHAPTANG

Steamed Clams & Clam Soup

STEAMED CLAMS

4 large or 12 regular clams, scrubbed with a
   brush and soaked in salty water 20 minutes
$1/4$ cup (60 ml) boiling water
Liberal sprinkling of white pepper
$1^1/2$ teaspoons very finely chopped garlic
$1/2$ teaspoon sesame oil
$1/4$ teaspoon sugar
1 egg, hard boiled, yolk and white separated
   (press the egg yolk and egg white separately
   through a coarse sieve, and set aside)
Chopped parsley and red chili, for garnishing

Put the clams and boiling water in a wok and bring back to the boil. Cook, stirring several times, just until the clams have started to open. Hold each clam shell over a bowl and prise open with a sharp knife, reserving the juice. Remove the clam meat, discarding the small dark area. If using very large clams, finely chop the remaining clam meat and transfer to the bowl with the juice; smaller clams can be left whole.

Place the clams on a heat-proof plate. Sprinkle each clam with a little pepper, garlic, sesame oil, and sugar. Just before serving, steam the clams for 5 minutes; chop or leave whole as desired. Plate the sieved egg as a garnish or topping, then add more chopped clam meat on top. Garnish clams with parsely and chili; serve as an appetizer or as part of a meal with rice.

CLAM SOUP

4 cups (1 liter) water
$2^1/2$ lb ($1^1/4$ kg) small clams, scrubbed
2 oz (60 g) long white radish, very
   thinly sliced
1 large red chili, seeded and sliced
1 oz (30 g) mung bean sprouts (optional)
4 cloves garlic, smashed and shopped
$1/2$ teaspoon very finely grated ginger
Liberal grinding of black pepper
1 teaspoon crushed dried chili (optional)
Salt to taste
2 tablespoons chopped scallions (spring onion)

Bring the water to a boil and add the clams. Simmer until the clams open. Add radish, chilies, bean sprouts, garlic, ginger, pepper, and dried chili. Simmer 3 to 5 minutes, then taste and add salt, if desired.

Transfer to a serving dish and garnish with scallion.

OJING-OH BOKEUM

Stir-fried Spicy Squid

Simple to prepare and guaranteed to please. ☻ ☻

1 lb 3 oz (600 g) squid
3 tablespoons vegetable oil
3 cloves garlic, smashed and finely chopped
$1/2$ teaspoon finely grated fresh ginger
1 small onion, very thinly sliced
1–2 large green chilies, seeded and thinly sliced
1–2 large red chilies, seeded and thinly sliced
1 small carrot, julienned
1 tablespoon Korean chili paste (*gochujang*)
$1^1/_2$ tablespoons light soy sauce
2–3 teaspoons chili powder
1 tablespoon sugar
1 teaspoon salt
2 teaspoons sesame oil
Black and white sesmae seeds to garnish

Pull the head off each squid and cut off the tentacles just above the eyes, push out the hard, beaky portion in the centre, and discard. Remove the skin from the squid and cut the hoods in bite-sized pieces. Rinse and pat both hoods and tentacles dry with paper towel.

Heat the oil in a wok and add the garlic, ginger, and onion. Stir-fry over high heat for about 30 seconds, then add the squid, chilies, carrot, and chili paste. Stir-fry over high head until the squid turns white and is just cooked, about 2 minutes. Add the soy sauce, chilli powder, sugar, salt, and sesame oil. Toss to mix well, then transfer to a serving dish. Do not overcook the squid or it will become tough.

Garnish with black and white sesame seeds.

KKOTGETANG

Crab and Vegetable Hotpot

A delicious, warming seafood dish, ideal for cold winter evenings. ⏱

2 lb (1 kg) raw blue swimmer crab
4 clams, scrubbed with a brush
5 tablespoons Korean chili paste (*gochujang*)
8 cups (2 liters) water
1$\frac{1}{2}$ teaspoons salt
6 cloves garlic, smashed and chopped
1 small leek, white part only thinly sliced
$\frac{1}{2}$ red bell pepper (capsicum), julienned
$\frac{1}{2}$ green bell pepper (capsicum), julienned
2 scallions (spring onions), sliced
1–2 teaspoons chili powder
2 tablespoons chopped fresh cilantro
   (coriander) leaves
Fresh crown daisy, for garnishing

Remove the back from the crab and wash, discarding any spongey matter. Cut the crab into 4 pieces, cracking the legs with a cleaver. Set aside.

Simmer the clams in water until they just begin to open, set aside.

Put the chili paste, water, and salt in a large saucepan and bring to a boil. Cover, lower heat, and simmer 10 minutes. Add the crab and clams and simmer with the pan uncovered for 5 minutes. Add the garlic, leek, bell pepper, scallion, and chili powder. Simmer until crab is cooked, about 5 minutes.

Scatter with fresh cilantro or crown daisy and serve with rice and other dishes, such as fried dried pollack and pan-fried green chili.

DAK JJIM & DAKDORITANG

Stuffed Chicken with Ginseng & Spicy Chicken Stew

STUFFED CHICKEN WITH GINSENG

This chicken is best prepared using a pressure cooker, but it can also be simmered gently in a saucepan with a tight-fitting lid. ☻

> 1 chicken weighing $1^1/_2$–2 lb ($^3/_4$–1 kg)
> 4 dried chestnuts, soaked in water 30 minutes
> 3 jujubes (dried red dates)
> 2 cloves garlic, left whole
> $1^1/_2$ teaspoons salt
> $1^3/_4$ cups (400 ml) water
> 2 pieces dried ginseng, about 3 in (8 cm) long

Dak Jjim (Stuffed Chicken with Ginseng) (top) and Dakdoritang (Spicy Chicken Stew) (bottom).

Wash and dry the chicken inside and out. Mix the chestnuts, jujubes, garlic, and $^1/_2$ teaspoon of the salt in a bowl, then put these inside the chicken. Close the cavity of the chicken by threading a skewer in and out of the flap. Put the chicken in a pressure cooker and add water, the remaining teaspoon of salt and ginseng. Close the cooker and bring up to pressure. Cook for 20 minutes, then reduce pressure but keeping cooking the chicken for another 10 minutes or until the chicken is very tender. Serve whole or in pieces with the ginseng. If using a saucepan, turn the chicken several times during cooking to ensure it cooks evenly. Simmer with the lid firmly closed for 1 to $1^1/_4$ hours, adding a little more water if necessary.

SPICY CHICKEN STEW ☻

> 2 lb (1 kg) chicken pieces (with the bone), cut into bite-sized portions
> 1 portion Spicy Chicken Stew Marinade (see recipe on page 31)
> 4 cups (1 liter) water
> 13 oz (400 g) potatoes, cut in $1^3/_4$-in (4-cm) chunks
> $6^1/_2$ oz (200 g) carrots, quartered lengthways, halved across
> 3 jujubes (dried red dates)
> 2 medium onions, each cut in 6 wedges
> $3^1/_2$ oz (100 g) leek, white part only, very thinly sliced
> 1 large green chili, seeded and sliced
> 1 large red chili, seeded and sliced
> Salt to taste
> 2 teaspoons sesame oil
> Sesame seeds to garnish

Heat a wok, then add chicken to the dry wok, and stir over medium heat for 2 minutes. Transfer to a bowl. Prepare marinade and pour over chicken, stirring to mix well. Marinate 5 minutes. Transfer chicken and marinade to a pan; add water. Bring to a boil, cover, lower heat, and simmer 15 minutes. Add the potatoes, jujubes, and carrots and simmer until tender, 20 to 25 minutes, stirring several times. Add onions, leek, and chilies and simmer 5 minutes. Add salt to taste and sprinkle with sesame oil and seeds.

SAMGYETANG

Chicken Stuffed with Rice and Ginseng

Ginseng, one of Korea's most famous products, gives a special flavor as well as medicinal value to the filling of glutinous rice, jujubes (dried red dates), and chestnuts. You can use two spring chickens or one large chicken for this dish. ☉

2 spring chickens (Cornish hens), about 1 lb (450 g) each, or 1 chicken weighing about 2 lb (1 kg)
$1/2$ cup (100 g) glutinous rice, soaked in warm water 30 minutes, drained
2 pieces dried ginseng, each about 2 in (5 cm) long
6 dried jujubes (dried red dates)
2 dried chestnuts, soaked in water 30 minutes, coarsely chopped (optional)
$1^1/2$ teaspoons salt
Liberal sprinkling white pepper
2 thin slices fresh ginger
2 cloves garlic, halved lengthways
1 scallion (spring onion), finely sliced

Dip
1 tablespoon salt
1 teaspoon freshly ground black pepper

Wash and dry the chickens and clean inside. Combine rice, ginseng, 4 jujubes, chestnuts and $1/2$ teaspoon of the salt in a bowl, stirring to mix. If using spring chickens, divide the mixture between the two, ensuring each chicken has 1 piece of ginseng and 2 jujubes. If using one larger chicken, put all the rice mixture inside. Do not pack the chickens too tightly with the mixture, as it will swell during cooking. Close the cavity of the chicken by threading a skewer in and out of the flap several times.

Place the spring chickens or chicken in a saucepan just large enough to hold them, then add water to just cover. Add the 1 teaspoon salt, pepper, 2 jujubes, ginger, garlic, and scallion and bring to a boil. Cover, lower the heat, and simmer gently for 30 minutes. Turn and cook until very tender and the flesh is almost falling off the bone, 20 to 30 minutes for spring chickens and 30 to 40 minutes for the whole chicken.

To serve, halve the spring chickens or cut larger chicken in quarters. Return the chicken and filling to the soup and serve. If preferred, the chicken and rice can be served together, with the soup in separate small bowls. Serve with the **dip**, made by combining salt and pepper and, if liked, small bowls of kimchi.

DAKKOCHI GUI & SANJEOK

Skewered Pan-Fried Chicken & Beef and Vegetable Skewers

SKEWERED PAN-FRIED CHICKEN

4 oz (120 g) chicken thigh fillet or breast, cut in 8
8 winter or pine mushrooms, or small button mushrooms
3–4 scallions (spring onions), cut in 1^1/$_2$-in (3-cm) lengths
1 red bell pepper (capsicum), cut to the same size as the scallion
4 bamboo skewers
1 portion Bulgogi Marinade (see recipe on page 31)
2 tablespoons vegetable oil

Marinade for chicken

2 teaspoons sesame oil
1 clove garlic, smashed and very finely chopped
^{1}/$_4$ teaspoon very finely grated fresh ginger
Liberal sprinkling of white pepper

Put the chicken in a small bowl and add all chicken marinade ingredients, tossing to mix well. Set aside for 5 minutes. Thread the 2 pieces of chicken, 2 mushrooms, alternating with scallion and the bell pepper, onto each of 4 skewers. Prepare the **Bulgogi Marinade** and pour over skewers. Marinate for 5 minutes, then remove the skewers; boil the marinade in a small saucepan for 2 to 3 mintues, then transfer to 4 sauce bowls. Heat the oil in a skillet and fry the skewers over medium heat, turning to cook evenly, until done, about 5 minutes. Serve skewers with the marinade as a dip.

BEEF AND VEGETABLE SKEWERS

3^1/$_2$ oz (100 g) oyster mushrooms
3^1/$_2$ oz (100 g) fresh *shiitake* mushrooms
5^1/$_2$ oz (160 g) beef sirloin, cut in ^{1}/$_2$-in (1-cm) slices, 3 in (7 cm) long
2 oz (60 g) scallion (spring onions), cut in 3-in (7-cm) lengths
1 portion Bulgogi Marinade (see recipe on page 31)
2 tablespoons vegetable oil

Cut mushroom caps cut in ^{1}/$_2$-in (1-cm) wide slices, discarding the stems. Thread the mushroom slices, meat and scallion onto bamboo skewers, alternating.

Prepare the **Bulgogi Marinade**. Place skewers in a dish; cover with marinade for 10 minutes. Remove skewers and drain. Heat oil in a skillet and cook the skewers, turning until done.

Helpful hint: Both dishes can be grilled; turn the skewers frequently until cooked.

YUKHOE

Raw Beef Salad

A simple and satisfying salad of thin raw beef slices with crunchy vegetables. ☺

6$^1\!/_2$ oz (200 g) beef fillet, trimmed of all fat
4–6 lettuce leaves, washed and drained
1 tablespoon pine nuts, ground to a powder
1–2 cloves garlic, very thinly sliced
$^1\!/_4$ Asian pear (*nashi*), finely julienned
1 teaspoon lime or lemon juice
1 teaspoon sesame oil
1 egg yolk (optional)
Pine nuts, for garnishing

Sauce
1 tablespoon soy sauce
2 teaspoons sugar
$^1\!/_2$ teaspoon smashed and finely chopped garlic
1 teaspoon sesame seed, toasted and coarsely crushed
1 teaspoon chili powder (optional)
Liberal grinding black pepper

Chill the beef in the freezer for 30 minutes, then slice very thinly. Combine all ingredients for the **sauce** and add the beef, tossing to mix well. Set aside.

Line a plate with lettuce leaves. Shape the marinated beef into a mound and place in the center of the plate and scatter with pine nuts and garlic. Toss the pear with lime juice and arrange around the beef. Put the egg yolk in a small sauce bowl and use as a dip for the beef if desired.

GALBI GUI & GALBI JJIM

Grilled Beef Ribs & Stewed Beef Ribs

GRILLED BEEF RIBS ⏱

1¹/₂–2 lb (³/₄–1 kg) beef short ribs, cut in
   1¹/₂-in (4-cm) lengths

Marinade
¹/₄ cup (60 ml) light soy sauce
¹/₄ cup (40 g) soft brown sugar
1¹/₂ tablespoons sesame oil
1¹/₂ tablespoon very finely chopped garlic
1¹/₂ tablespoons rice wine
¹/₄ teaspoon freshly ground black pepper
1 scallion (spring onion), finely chopped
¹/₂ cup (125 ml) beef stock (see recipe on page 31)

Galbi Jjim (Stewed Beef Ribs) (left) and Galbi Gui (Grilled Beef Ribs) (right).

Put beef ribs in a bowl. Mix all **marinade** ingredients in a small bowl, then pour over the beef; massage with the hand for about 1 minute. Cover and leave to marinate for at least 4 hours.

Heat a grill or broiler and cook the ribs, turning to brown on both sides. Serve on a plate.

STEWED BEEF RIBS ⏱

1¹/₂–2 lb (³/₄–1 kg) beef ribs, cut in 1-in
   (2¹/₂-cm) pieces
3-in (8-cm) piece carrot
3-in (8-cm) piece long white radish
4 dried chestnuts, soaked in hot water for
   30 minutes
4 jujubes (dried red dates)
20 ginkgo nuts

Sauce
¹/₃ cup (85 ml) light soy sauce
2¹/₂ tablespoons rice wine
2¹/₂ tablespoons sesame oil
2 tablespoons sugar
6–8 cloves garlic, smashed and finely chopped
2 scallions (spring onions), finely chopped
Freshly ground pepper to taste
1 dried black *shiitake* mushroom, soaked in hot
   water to soften, cap finely shredded

Rinse beef ribs in cold water, then drain. Blanch in boiling water for 10 minutes, then transfer to a saucepan. Add water to cover the ribs, then add all the sauce ingredients. Bring to a boil, cover, lower heat, and simmer gently until the meat is tender. Cut carrot and radish into pieces the same size as the chestnuts, then add, together with the chestnuts, ginkgo nuts and jujubes. Simmer until tender. Serve hot with rice.

BULGOGI

Barbecued Seasoned Beef

Traditionally, *bulgogi* is made by cooking slices of marinated beef over a wood fire, but these days, it is more likely to be cooked on a table-top gas grill or on a metal or brass convex broiler. If you can barbecue the beef over wood or charcoal, you'll get that good old-fashioned flavor, but thanks to the excellent marinade, the meat will still taste good if cooked over gas or electricity, or even if it is pan-fried. ⊘

1¹/₂ lb (750 g) sirloin or rib eye beef, thinly
    sliced, cut in pieces about 2 x 4¹/₂ in
    (5 x 12 cm), excess fat removed
1 tablespoon vegetable oil
1 green bell pepper (capsicum), thinly sliced,
    or 1 large green chili, thinly sliced
1 medium onion, thinly sliced
6¹/₂ oz (200 g) button or fresh *shiitake*
    mushrooms, sliced (optional)

Marinade

1 tablespoon rice wine
¹/₂–1 Asian pear (*nashi*), grated to yield
    1 tablespoon pear juice (optional)
¹/₄ cup (60 ml) light soy sauce
2 tablespoons sesame oil
1 tablespoon soft brown sugar
1 tablespoon very finely chopped garlic
2 scallions (spring onions), finely chopped
¹/₂ cup (125 ml) beef stock (optional)

In a large bowl, mix the beef slices, rice wine, and pear juice thoroughly, massaging well with the hand for about 1 minute. Then, add all the other **marinade** ingredients. Cover and leave to marinate for 3 to 4 hours.

Heat a large skillet, drain the beef slices, and sear in the pan, without any oil, for 1 minute on each side, and set it aside. Next, heat the oil in the skillet and stir-fry the bell pepper, onion, and mushrooms over medium heat until cooked but still slightly firm, about 3 minutes. Add the meat and mix well.

Serve with the salad, Korean chili paste (*gochujang*), and rice.

Helpful hints: An alternative way of preparing this dish is to heat a barbecue or grill and cook the beef slices over high heat for about 1 minute on each side; prepare the vegetables as above, and mix in the meat when ready.

Koreans enjoy serving their grills with lettuce leaves, sesame leaves, sliced raw garlic, and sliced green chili on the side. Arrange these ingredients and the meat on a leaf, then wrap and dip the package in a spicy sauce before eating.

CHADOLPAKEE

Grilled Korean Beef Steak

This recipe for grilled beef couldn't be easier. Start with thinly sliced good quality beef steak, grill it on a table-top grill, and serve it with sesame oil, salt, and pepper. The result confirms the old saying that some of the simplest things in life are the best. ⏱

1 lb 3 oz (600 g) beef sirloin
1 tablespoon sesame oil
1 tablespoon salt
$1/4$ teaspoon freshly ground black pepper
4 cloves garlic, peeled and thinly sliced
(optional)

Chill the beef in the freezer for 30 minutes to make it easier to cut, then slice very thinly. Lay the slices on a plate. Combine sesame oil, salt, and pepper and divide between 4 small sauce dishes.

When it is time to serve, cook the garlic and beef to taste on a table-top grill and serve with the dip. Each person flavors a morsel of meat and roasted garlic with the dip before eating.

Helpful hints: Raw garlic is often eaten together with the meat. This recipe is also commonly used to prepare grilled beef tongue, a Korean delicacy.

JEYOOKBOKEUM

Spicy Stir-fried Pork

A dish so tasty, your guests will never imagine just how fast it is to prepare. ℗

2 tablespoons vegetable oil
13 oz (400 g) pork fillet or loin, thinly sliced
4 dried black *shiitake* mushrooms, soaked in warm water to soften, stems discarded, caps sliced
1–2 large red chilies, seeded and sliced
1–2 large green chilies, seeded and sliced
1 small onion, thinly sliced
1–2 scallions (spring onions), sliced
5 oz (125 g) kimchi, squeezed dry and finely sliced
1 tablespoon sesame seeds, toasted and coarsely crushed while still warm

Seasoning

4 tablespoons Korean chili paste (*gochujang*)
1–2 teaspoons chili powder
2 cloves garlic, smashed and finely chopped
1 teaspoon very finely grated fresh ginger
2 tablespoons water
$1^1/_2$ tablespoons light soy sauce
1 tablespoon sugar
2 teaspoons rice wine
2 teaspoons sesame oil

Prepare seasoning by combining all ingredients in a small bowl and stirring until sugar is dissolved.

Heat vegetable oil in a wok and add pork. Stir-fry over high heat for about 30 seconds, then add mushrooms, chilies, onion, scallions, and kimchi. Stir-fry for 1 minute, then add the seasoning sauce and continue stir-frying until the pork is cooked, about 3 minutes. Serve hot with steamed rice.

JAPCHAE

Transparent Noodles with Beef and Vegetables

This delicious noodle dish is ideal for lunch or any light meal. ✆

Beef

6$^1/_2$ oz (200 g) beef fillet or stirloin, shredded
1 tablespoon light soy sauce
1 tablespoon sugar
1 teaspoon sesame oil
1 teaspoon very finely chopped garlic
4–6 scallions (spring onions), cut in 1$^1/_2$-in (4-cm) lengths
1 tablespoon vegetable oil

Vegetables

2 tablespoons vegetable oil
2 onions, thinly sliced
4 dried black mushrooms, soaked to soften, stems discarded, caps shredded
4 wood-ear mushrooms, soaked to soften, then thinly sliced
1 medium carrot, finely julienned
$^1/_2$ green bell pepper (capsicum), finely julienned
$^1/_2$ red bell pepper (capsicum), finely julienned
1 tablespoon light soy sauce
$^1/_2$ cup (125 ml) water
$^1/_4$ teaspoon salt

Noodles

1 tablespoon oil
13 oz (400 g) potato-starch or cellophane noodles, soaked in warm water 10 minutes.

2 tablespoons sugar
1 tablespoon sesame oil
1 tablespoon soy sauce
1 teaspoon salt
$^1/_4$ teaspoon white pepper

To prepare the **beef**, put the meat in a bowl and add soy sauce, sugar, sesame oil, and garlic. Massage for about 1 minute, then leave to marinate 30 minutes. Heat vegetable oil in a wok, and stir-fry the beef over high heat until cooked. Transfer to a bowl.

To prepare the **vegetables**, heat the oil in a wok and add onions. Stir-fry over medium heat until transparent, then add mushrooms and stir-fry 2 minutes. Increase heat slightly and add carrot and both lots of bell pepper. Stir-fry 2 minutes, then sprinkle with soy sauce and salt. Add water and stir-fry until the vegetables are soft and the liquid has dried up. Transfer to the bowl with the beef.

To prepare the **noodles**, heat oil in a wok and add noodles, stirring for a few seconds to coat well with oil. Add sugar, sesame, soy, salt, and pepper, then add the reserved beef and vegetables, stirring to mix all ingredients thoroughly.

Transfer to 4 noodles bowls; serve immediately.

KALGUKSU

Noodle Soup with Vegetables

Quick and easy to prepare, this noodle soup makes for a satisfying meal. ☻

6 cups (1¹⁄₂ liters) Beef Stock (see recipe on page 31)
1 small potato, about 5 oz (150 g), peeled and diced
1 small piece zucchini (courgette), about 5 oz (150 g), peeled and julienned
12 to 20 small clams
Salt to taste
13 oz (400 g) fresh wheat noodles, or 250 g dried buckwheat noodles
Dried crushed chili to serve (optional)

Sauce

1 tablespoon soy sauce
1 tablespoon Beef Stock (see recipe on page 31)
1 teaspoon minced ginger
1 teaspoon chopped scallion (spring onion)
1 teaspoon seseame oil
1 teaspoon fried sesame seeds

Prepare the **sauce** by combining all the sauce ingredients. Transfer to a small sauce dish and set aside.

Heat the stock and add potato. Simmer until almost tender, then add zucchini and clams. Simmer until done, taste and add salt if desired. Keep warm.

If using fresh noodles, plunge into boiling water and cook 1 to 2 minutes, until done; dried noodles require about 4 minutes. Drain noodles and divide between 4 large noodle bowls. Add the soup and vegetables to the bowls containing the noodles and serve hot with crushed chili for adding to taste, together with the sauce.

MULNAEMGMYEON

Chilled Noodles with Beef and Salad

While a dish of chilled noodles may seem unusual to non-Asians, it is actually very refreshing. ✺

4 cups (1 liter) beef stock, preferably homemade
8 oz (250 g) brisket or chuck beef
1$^1/_2$ in (4 cm) ginger, sliced
1 medium onion, sliced
11$^1/_2$ oz (350 g) dried wheat or buckwheat noodles, simmered until just cooked, drained, and cooled in iced water
1 small Asian pear (*nashi*), peeled and sliced
2 hard-boiled eggs, halved lengthways
1 small slender cucumber, or $^1/_4$ regular cucumber, julienned in long strips, seasoned with a pinch of salt
$^1/_2$ small long white radish, julienned in long strips and seasoned with a pinch of chili powder, garlic, salt, and sesame seeds

Put beef stock, beef, ginger, and onion in a saucepan, bring to a boil, cover, and simmer until the beef is tender. Leave beef in the stock until cool, then slice thinly. Strain stock and chill both stock and beef in the fridge.

To serve, divide the noodles between 4 large bowls. Garnish with sliced beef, pear, and egg. Add some of the seasoned cucumber and radish strips to each serving. Pour over the chilled beef stock and serve immediately.

DOLSOT BIBIMBAP

Pot Rice with Fried Beef and Vegetables

Dolsot Bibimbap is a popular dish of steamed rice with vegetables and beef in a pot. Sometimes the *bimbimbap* is served without any side dishes. ② ②

3–4 tablespoons vegetable oil
4 dried black *shiitake* mushrooms, soaked in hot water to soften, and sliced; stems discarded
1 teaspoon salt
1 small zucchini (courgette), julienned
$6^{1}/_{2}$ oz (200 g) bracken, sliced and soaked 10 hours
2 teaspoons soy sauce
Small bundle soy bean sprouts, about $6^{1}/_{2}$ oz (200 g) tails cut off, or mung bean sprouts
$6^{1}/_{2}$ oz (200 g) minced beef
$6^{1}/_{2}$ oz (200 g) spinach, coarsely chopped
4 cups (600 g) hot cooked rice
4 tablespoons Korean chili paste (*gochujang*)
4 tablespoons shredded dried laver
1 tablespoon sesame seeds, toasted and coarsely crushed while still warm
2 teaspoons sesame oil

Heat 2 teaspoons oil in a wok and add the mushrooms. Stir-fry over medium heat until cooked, 3 to 4 minutes. Season with a pinch of salt, remove and drain on paper towel.

Add another 2 teaspoons of oil to the wok and stir-fry the zucchini, seasoning with a pinch of salt and 1 teaspoon soy sauce. Add 1 to 2 tablespoons water while stir-frying, and cook until the zucchini is tender and almost dry. Put on a dish and keep warm.

Add 2 teaspoons oil to the wok and stir-fry the soy bean sprouts over medium heat until cooked, 3 minutes. Season with a little salt and transfer to the dish with the other cooked vegetables.

Add 2 teaspoons oil to the wok and stir-fry the beef until cooked, seasoning with a pinch of salt and the remaining 1 teaspoon of soy sauce. Add to the plate and keep warm.

Add 1 teaspoon oil to the wok and stir-fry the spinach until cooked, 2 to 3 minutes, then season with a pinch of salt.

Divide hot rice between 4 bowls. Add $^{1}/_{2}$ to 1 teaspoon chili paste to each, and scatter each with laver, sesame seeds, and sesame oil. If preferred, add some of the mushrooms, zucchini, bean sprouts, beef, and spinach to each, or put the accompaniments on a plate in the center of the table for each person to take according to taste. Serve with the chili paste (*gochujang*).

Helpful hint: If desired, a fried egg could be added to the top of each portion of rice. If clay or other individual heat-proof casseroles are available, grease the inside of each lightly with oil, add rice and put over medium heat for 3 to 4 minutes before garnishing with the beef and vegetables.

KIMCHI BOKEUMBAP

Stir-fried Rice with Kimchi and Beef

This is a handy way of using left-over cooked rice, which can be kept refrigerated in a covered container. (In fact, it's preferable for all fried rice dishes that the rice is kept overnight, so that it is completely dry.) The rice is stir-fried with shredded beef, spicy kimchi, onion, scallion, and garlic, and seasoned with soy sauce and sesame oil for a quickly made and very tasty dish ideal for lunch or a light supper. ☻

6½ oz (200 g) beef sirloin, finely shredded
1 tablespoon sesame oil
1½ tablespoons soy sauce
1–2 teaspoons very finely chopped garlic
2 tablespoons vegetable oil
1 small onion, finely chopped
1 green chili, sliced into small pieces
1 scallion (spring onion), coarsely chopped
1½ cups firmly packed (300 g) chopped *kimchi*
3 cups (450 g) cold cooked rice
Black sesame seeds to garnish

Put beef in a bowl and sprinkle with 1 tablespoon of the sesame oil. Add the soy sauce and garlic, mix well and leave beef to season for 5 minutes.

Heat ½ tablespoon of the oil in a wok then add beef and stir-fry over very high heat until cooked, about 1 minute. Remove from wok and set aside.

Reduce heat to medium, add 1 tablespoon of the remaining vegetable oil to the wok and when hot, add onion, chili, and scallion. Stir-fry until onion softens, 1 to 2 minutes, then add kimchi and stir-fry 1 minute. Remove from wok and set aside.

Increase heat to maximum and add remaining 1 tablespoon vegetable oil. When hot, add rice and stir-fry over high heat for 1 minute. Return beef and kimchi mixture to the wok and continue stir-frying until heated through. Transfer to a serving bowl and sprinkle with the remaining tablespoon of sesame oil. Garnish with sesame seeds.

SONGPYEON

Korean Thanksgiving Cakes

These traditional cakes made of rice-flour dough contain a filling of chopped sweetened chestnuts and green mung beans. To save time, you could used canned sweetened chestnuts or sweet chestnut purée. If possible, place the cakes on a bed of pine needles so that the delicious aroma will give a subtle flavor to the cakes during steaming. ⏰⏰⏰

3 cups (600 g) rice flour
$^1/_4$ teaspoon salt
$^3/_4$–1 cup (185–250 ml) water
$^1/_3$ cup (60 g) green mung beans, simmered in water until very soft, drained
$1^1/_2$ tablespoons sugar
10 cooked sweetened chestnuts, coarsely mashed chopped
Fresh pine needles (optional)
1 tablespoon sesame oil

Put rice flour in a bowl and stir in $^3/_4$ cup (185 ml) water, gradually adding more as needed to get a smooth, non-sticky dough. (If the dough seems too wet to work with, add a little more rice flour.)

Put the mung beans in a bowl and mix with sugar. Add the sweetened chestnuts and mix.

Take about 1 heaped tablespoon of dough and shape into a ball. Flatten into a circle 3 to $3^1/_2$ in (8 to 9 cm) across, then put a heaped teaspoon of the mung bean and chestnut filling in the center.

Squeeze edges to enclose the filling. When all the dough has been used up, place the cakes in a single layer on a plate lined, if possible, with pine needles. If these are not available, brush the plate with sesame oil before placing on the cakes. Steam over boiling water until cooked, about 30 minutes. Brush the top of each cake with sesame oil and serve warm or at room temperature. This makes about 24 rice cakes.

Helpful hints: The dough may be colored with colors of your choice. If canned sweetened chestnuts are not available, put 10 dried chestnuts in a bowl, cover with boiling water and stand 30 minutes. Discard the water, then put in a saucepan, cover with water, and simmer until the chestnuts are soft, about 45 minutes. Chop finely and sprinkle with 1 tablespoon honey.

YAK KWA

Fried Korean Cookies

These unusual cookies are made from a pastry-like dough, where sesame oil replaces butter and the subtle flavoring is provided by fresh ginger juice, honey and rice wine. The deep-fried cookies are dipped in a sugar and honey syrup, and sprinkled with cinnamon and pine nuts. Serve them warm and see them disappear quickly. ✆✆

1¹/₂ tablespoons finely chopped fresh ginger
1 tablespoons water
2 cups (250 g) all-purpose (plain) flour
Pinch of salt
3 tablespoons sesame oil
3 tablespoons honey
2 tablespoons rice wine
Vegetable oil for deep-frying
Cinnamon powder
1 tablespoon crushed pine nuts

Syrup
¹/₂ cup (125 ml) water
¹/₄ cup (60 g) sugar
¹/₄ cup (60 g) honey
Pinch of salt

Make the **syrup** by bringing water, sugar, honey, and salt to a boil in a saucepan, stirring frequently. Simmer 1 minute, then remove from the heat.

Blend the ginger and water in a spice grinder, then press firmly in a sieve to obtain the ginger juice. Set aside.

Put flour and salt in a bowl and sprinkle over the sesame oil. Stir to mix, then rub with the fingertips as when making a pastry. When the texture is sandy, add honey, rice wine, and 1¹/₂ to 2 tablespoons water to make a pliable dough. Turn out dough onto a lightly floured board and roll out until about ¹/₄ in (5 mm) thick. Cut into shapes with a cookie cutter.

Heat oil for deep-frying in a wok and fry the cookies, a few at a time, over medium heat until cooked and golden brown, 2 to 3 minutes; do not have the oil too hot or the cookies will brown before they are cooked through. Drain on paper towel. Hold each cookie in a pair of tongs and dip into the syrup, turning to coat it well.

Place the cookies on a plate, garnish with a sprinkling of cinnamon and pine nuts if desired.

HWAJEON & YEONCI

Pan-fried Rice Dough Cakes & Persimmon Sherbet

PAN-FRIED RICE DOUGH CAKES ⏱

2 cups (320 g) rice flour
$\frac{1}{2}$ teaspoon salt
$1\frac{1}{2}$ cups (375 ml) warm water
$\frac{1}{2}$ cup (125 ml) vegetable oil
$\frac{1}{2}$ cup (125 ml) honey
20 azalea flowers or daisies, washed and dried

Mix rice flour, salt, and water to make a smooth, pliable but non-sticky dough. Break off about 1 tablespoon of dough, then pat with the fingers to make a circle about $2\frac{1}{4}$ in (6 cm) across. Alternatively, transfer the dough to a floured surface, roll out to about $\frac{1}{2}$ in (1 cm) thick, and use a cookie cutter or a drinking glass to cut out the pancakes.

Heat oil to cover the bottom of a skillet and when hot, put in several cakes, lower heat, and fry until golden brown underneath, about 2 to 3 minutes. Then turn and cook the other side, if you wish to brown it even more.

Drain on paper towel, then put on a serving plate and drizzle with honey. Garnish each cake with a flower.

PERSIMMON SHERBET ⏱

This is an all-natural refreshing dessert, and tastes like a sweet, soft, and chilled custard.

4 fresh ripe but firm persimmons

Wash each persimmon and wipe dry. Put in the deep-freeze and leave until solid. When serving, serve whole or cut each persimmon into quarters and put on a small plate.

INSAM-CHA & SUJEONGGWA

Ginseng Tea & Persimmon Tea

GINSENG TEA

Ginseng is Korea's most famous product, a medicinal root whose amazing properties have been known for around 5,000 years. ⏱

1²/₃ oz (50 g) dried ginseng root
4 jujubes (dried red dates)
8 cups (2 liters) water
¹/₃ cup (85 g) sugar, or more to taste
1 tablespoon pine nuts

Put ginseng, jujubes, and water in a large saucepan. Bring to a boil, cover, reduce heat to minimum and cook very gently for 4 hours. Add sugar and stir to dissolve. Pour through a strainer into glasses or porcelain tea bowls, and serve with a few pine nuts floating on the top.

Helpful hint: Although top quality, whole aged Korean ginseng root is very expensive, packets of younger creamy white dried rootlets (available in Chinese medicine shops and most Asian stores) are moderately priced and ideal for this recipe.

PERSIMMON TEA ⏱

2 4-in (10-cm) cinnamon sticks
1¹/₂ in (4 cm) fresh ginger, thinly sliced
4 black peppercorns
4 jujubes (dried red dates)
6 cups (1¹/₂ liters) water
3 tablespoons sugar, or more to taste
12 pine nuts
4 dried persimmons, soaked in water 30 minutes, drained (chopped if desired)

Put cinnamon sticks, ginger, peppercorns, jujubes, and water into a large saucepan and bring to a boil. Cover, lower heat and simmer for 1 hour. Add sugar to taste and stir until dissolved. Pour the mixture through a sieve into a bowl and add the dried persimmons. Allow to cool, then refrigerate until chilled. When serving, divide the liquid between 4 bowls or glasses and add some pine nuts and a whole dried persimmon (or chopped persimmon) to each serving.

Modeum Jeon
Pan-fried Beef, Fish, and Zucchini

The photograph of Modeum Jeon appears on page 41. ⏱

- 8 oz (250 g) beef tenderloin or striploin, thinly cut in round slices
- 8 oz (250 g) white fish fillet, thinly cut in round slices
- 1–2 fat zucchini (courgettes), thinly sliced
- 1 teaspoon salt
- Liberal sprinkling white pepper
- $^3/_4$ cup (90 g) all-purpose (plain) flour
- Vegetable oil for shallow frying
- 2 eggs, lightly beaten

Dipping Sauce
- 4 tablespoons light soy sauce
- 2 tablespoons vinegar
- 1–2 teaspoons very finely chopped garlic
- 1–2 red chilies, finely chopped

Combine ingredients for dipping sauce and divide between 4 small sauce bowls.

Sprinkle beef, fish, and zucchini with salt and pepper. Put flour in a plastic bag and add beef. Hold the top of the bag closed and gently shake to coat the beef with flour. Transfer to a sieve or colander and shake gently to dislodge excess flour. Repeat for the fish and zucchini.

Heat the oil in a wok. When it is moderately hot, dip the floured beef in beaten egg, then add to the oil. Cook, stirring several times, until brown all over, 1 to 2 minutes. Drain on paper towel. Repeat for the fish and zucchini. Transfer to a serving dish and serve hot with the dipping sauce.

Oisobaegi • *Stuffed Cucumber Kimchi*

The photograph of Oisobaegi appears on page 55. ⏱

- 3 small slender cucumbers, or 1 regular cucumber
- 5 tablespoons coarse salt

Filling
- $^1/_4$ small Asian pear (*nashi*), very finely julienned; if unavailable double the amount of long white radish or scallion (spring onion)
- 2-in (5-cm) piece long white radish, very finely julienned
- 1 scallion (spring onion), finely chopped
- 1 tablespoon very finely chopped garlic
- 1 teaspoon finely grated fresh ginger
- 1 tablespoon sugar
- 2 teaspoons chili powder or 1 tablespoon crushed dried chili

Cut lengthways slits down the center of each cucumber, but do not cut completely in half. If using a large cucumber, make 2 lengthways slits. Cut the cucumbers across into 2 1/2-in (6-cm) lengths. Rub salt outside the unpeeled cucumbers and push it inside the slits. Put cucumbers in a bowl, cover, and leave at room temperature for about 6 hours, until the cucumbers are soft.

Sikhye • *Rice and Barley Punch*

The photograph of Rice and Barley Punch appears on page 117. ☉

$^1/_3$ cup (60 g) barley, washed and drained
6 cups (1$^1/_2$ liters) water
2 tablespoons raw rice
4 thin slices fresh ginger
4 tablespoons sugar, or more to taste
12 pine nuts

Put barley and water in saucepan and bring to a boil. Cover, lower heat, and simmer very gently for 2 hours. Sieve, discarding the barley and saving the water.

Boil rice in a little water until cooked, then drain. Put the rice in a vacuum flask or rice cooker and add the strained barley water. Close the vacuum flask or set the rice cooker on "warm." Leave until the rice grains float, 3 to 4 hours.

Sieve the liquid into a saucepan. Rinse the rice grains under running water, transfer to a covered container and refrigerate. Bring the liquid to a boil with ginger and sugar, stirring several times. Simmer 10 minutes, remove ginger, allow to cool, then refrigerate. To serve, add some of the chilled rice grains and pine nuts to a bowl or glass of the chilled liquid.

Special Thanks
The publisher would like to thank all the people involved in the production of this publication, especially the management, chefs, and staff of The Shilla Hotel, Seoul, Korea. Special thanks to Ae Kyoung Han (Korean project coordinator), Ong Kiat Kim, and Yaeko Masuda for their kind assistance.

The publisher would also like to thank the following for the loan of their china, cutlery, glassware, and linen for the photographic shoot:

Art & Life (822-511-1100)
Kwang Ju Yo (822-3446-6543)
Ceramic Yo (822-546-2710)
Gana Art Shop (822-734-1019)
Korea Craft Promotion Foundation "Jeom"
  (822-733-9040)
Kyung-in Museum (822-733-4448)
Off Time (822-546-8915)
Room & Deco (822-585-8106)
Seven Dragon (822-586-7026)
  www.minsokpoom.com
St. Bless (822-3446-1442)
Sun Gallery (822-725-1735)
Thoart (822-732-3044)
U ri gu rut RYU (822-549-7573)
Wooil Yo (822-763-2562)
Yelang Ceramic (822-537-9931)

INDEX

Periplus World Cookbooks

TRAVEL THE WORLD IN YOUR KITCHEN!

Welcome to the world's best-selling international cookery series—and the first comprehensive encyclopaedia of world cooking! Each volume contains over 70 easy-to-follow recipes gathered in the country of origin. Introductory essays by noted food writers explore the cuisine's cultural roots and all food photographs are taken on location to ensure absolute authenticity. Truly the ultimate cookbooks for globetrotting gourmets!

"The scope of this library of books transcends the size of its volumes…They are thoughtful, well-planned, well-edited, and most importantly they strive mightily for authenticity, an effort sadly lacking in so many of today's 'ethnic' cookery books."

– "A Gourmet At Large" *Gourmet Magazine*, USA

The Food of Australia
ISBN 962 593 393 X Hardcover

The Food of Bali
ISBN 962 593 385 9 Hardcover

The Food of Jamaica
ISBN 962 593 228 3 Hardcover

The Food of Japan
ISBN 962 593 392 1 Hardcover

The Food of North Italy
ISBN 962 593 505 3 Hardcover

The Food of Paris
ISBN 962 593 991 1 Hardcover

The Food of Sante Fe
ISBN 962 593 229 1 Hardcover

The Food of Texas
ISBN 962 593 534 7 Hardcover